The Scottish
RAILWAY STORY

EDINBURGH : HMSO

Front cover: Scottish Railway Preservation
Society's 'Maude' crosses the Forth Railway Bridge

Back cover: Building the Forth Railway Bridge.
Workmen on a viaduct pier (BR/FOR/4/34/334)

Title page: North British Railway Company servants (BR/NBR/4/315)

ISBN 0 11 494187 4

ACKNOWLEDGEMENTS

The Scottish Record Office is grateful to the British Railways Board for permission to reproduce a large number of documents and photographs from the Scottish railway archives held in the Scottish Record Office and to the following for permission to reproduce items from their Collections: Mr W E Boyd, Messrs Dundas and Wilson, CS, Messrs Hill and Robb, Solicitors, the Mitchell Library, Glasgow, and the Royal Commission on the Ancient and Historical Monuments of Scotland. Thanks are also due to Mr Graham Dick for his help in selecting the photograph of Colinton Station. Prints of original photographs in the Scottish Record Office holdings were provided through the photographic services of the National Library of Scotland.

I am happy to record my personal gratitude to my colleague Mr George R Barbour whose profound knowledge of the railway records and railway history saved me from many pitfalls, technical and historical, and who identified a number of important items which have been included. Any factual errors that remain are my own.

Margaret H B Sanderson

INTRODUCTION

t he coming of the Railways was one of the most exciting developments of the 19th century. The transport revolution came to be dominated by the train, while speedier movement of raw materials and goods helped in turn to release the full potential of the industrial revolution itself. In human terms the effects of the Railways were enormous. Building the lines, locomotives and rolling stock called for both engineering skills and hard labour. Running the railway systems for the public created a vast range of new jobs and communities whose lives were bound up with the railways. For most people, however, the trains meant hitherto undreamed-of travel opportunities and an exciting new dimension to holidays, long or short. Rivalry between railway companies for a share of the travelling public created a flood of publicity material and literature.

The Scottish archives of the British Railways Board which were formerly housed in the British Transport Historical Records Department at 23 Waterloo Place, Edinburgh, passed to the Secretary of State for Scotland in terms of the Transport Act, 1968, and are now preserved in the Scottish Record Office. The present selection of documents from this rich archive, and from the deposited Collections of certain railway historians and others, emphasises the social effects of the railways in the age of steam, but tribute is also paid to the locomotives and other technical products of engineering skill.

The Archive Unit is intended as a study tool for use in schools, illustrating the transport revolution and social changes of the 19th and early 20th centuries and as a source of enjoyment for those who are interested in all aspects of railway history. The documents and photographs largely speak for themselves but explanatory notes, commentary and introductory passages to the main themes are provided. As study material the Unit should be used in association with the many available books on railway history and the experiences afforded by the activities of railway museums and societies.

NOTE ON THE USE OF THE PUBLICATION
The copies of documents and photographs are made available solely for use in schools or for private study. No further copying of the material or other use of the Unit, including use in publications of any kind, must be undertaken without first contacting the Scottish Record Office.

The Scottish railway archives may be consulted at West Register House, Charlotte Square, Edinburgh, where the West Search Room is open, Mon-Fri 9.00-4.45; closed certain public holidays and part of November for stocktaking. Information on the education services of the Scottish Record Office is available on request.

The Scottish Record Office
HM General Register House
Princes Street
Edinburgh EH1 3YY
Tel: 031-556 6585

ALSO AVAILABLE
SRO   Archive Unit I: The Coalminers
        Archive Unit 2: The First World War
        (Details on request)

CONTENTS

PART 1

The Coming of the Railways

he industrial revolution of the 18th and 19th centuries was accompanied from its earliest stages by an expansion of communications and transport systems in the form of new roads, bridges, canals and harbours.

The railways soon joined and eventually came to dominate this transport revolution. The earliest railways were iron railroads for horsedrawn wagons which were primarily constructed in order to move the increasing output of the coalmines to industrial consumers in Fife and the central belt of Scotland. They were originally built on the territories of landowners who saw them as an important new economic investment in their property and a speedy way of transporting the minerals found on their estates.

By the 1820s many of these wagonways had ceased to be privately owned, but with their directors and shareholders and authorised by parliament they became public companies. Traffic on some of them, including the Kilmarnock and Troon Railway continued to be horsedrawn until the 1840s. The Kilmarnock and Troon Railway was also the earliest line to carry passengers on a regular basis.

1
Rules for the Kilmarnock and Troon Iron Railway, printed from the Minutes of the Company, 4 October 1811. The Railway, the first Scottish railway to obtain a private Act of Parliament (1808), opened on 6 July 1812. Its original purpose was the conveyance of coal from the Duke of Portland's mines near Kilmarnock to Troon harbour. However, passengers were carried soon after the opening. The Company's Minute Book, 1808-1830, is the earliest railway minute book in the Scottish historical records of the British Railways Board. (BR/KTR/1/1)

KILMARNOCK and TROON IRON RAILWAY.

BYE-LAWS, RULES, ORDERS, AND REGULATIONS,

TO BE OBSERVED

By all Persons employed in Conveying any Goods, or other things, upon the Kilmarnock and Troon Iron Railway;

As established by the Company of Proprietors of the said Railway, under their common Seal, pursuant to the Directions contained in the Act of Parliament for the Incorporation of the said Company.

IT IS ORDERED,

I. THAT all Loaded Waggons or other Carriages employed on, or using the said Railway, proceeding from Kilmarnock to the Troon, shall on all occasions when the double road is completed, take, use, and proceed on the right hand track or road of the said RAILWAY; and that the Drivers, or other persons attending or conducting the same, shall in all cases take, use, and proceed in the middle path; and that every person offending against this Rule or Order, shall for every such offence, forfeit and pay to the said Company any sum not exceeding twenty shillings, nor less than five shillings. But, that during the present unfinished state of the Road, they shall be bound in all cases, to proceed in such tracks, as the Surveyor of the Road, by Notices to be fixed on Posts or otherways, may direct, under the same penalty for non-compliance as is herein before directed.

II. That no Waggon or other Carriage on, or conducted along the said RAILWAY, shall, on any account or pretext whatsoever, be turned or driven off the proper road or track, or made to pass from one track of the said RAILWAY to the other, except at the regular and proper places constructed for enabling such Waggons or other Carriages to turn out and pass each other; and that every person offending against this Rule or Order, shall, for every such offence, forfeit and pay to the said Company any sum not exceeding twenty shillings, nor less than five shillings.

III. That so soon as proper Weighing Machines shall have been constructed on the line of the RAILWAY, every Waggon used upon the said RAILWAY shall not only have the Owner's Name painted upon it, but also the weight of the said Waggon, in the same manner as the name of the Owner is directed to be painted on each waggon by the said Act.

IV. That the Owner of every Waggon or other Carriage employed on, or using the said RAILWAY, shall keep every such waggon or other carriage in good and perfect order and condition for working on the said RAILWAY, so as not to be liable to injure or damage the same, and so that the Wheels and Axles of every such waggon or other carriage be in true and perfect positions, and the opposite wheels confined to such a distance, as that the centre of the tread of one wheel to the centre of the tread of the other wheel, shall not exceed four feet four inches,

nor be less than four feet three inches; and that such wheels shall not exceed three feet in height; and no waggon or other carriage shall be suffered to pass on the said RAILWAY, unless the same shall be kept in such perfect order and condition as aforesaid; and that every person offending against this Rule or Order, shall for every such offence, forfeit and pay to the said Company any sum not exceeding forty shillings, nor less than twenty shillings.

V. And if at any time a waggon or waggons, or carriage or carriages, by accident or otherwise, be drawn off the road, or proper track, the Driver shall immediately stop until the same be placed in the proper road or track; but, if it is known, or can be proved, that he has dragged a waggon or waggons, carriage or carriages but one lineal yard after the same is out of its true road or track, he shall for every such offence forfeit and pay to the said Company any sum not exceeding twenty shillings, nor less than ten shillings.

VI. That no waggon or other carriage employed on, or using the said RAILWAY, shall be suffered or permitted to carry a greater quantity or weight of lading, than will make the aggregate amount of the weight of such lading, and of such waggon or other carriage taken together, two tons and a half legal weight, and that the owner of every such waggon or other carriage carrying any greater weight, unless in conveying any one article, which may happen to exceed the weight above described, shall forfeit and pay to the said Company for every hundred pounds over and above such allowed weight, any sum not exceeding twenty shillings, nor less than ten shillings.

VII. That no Driver or other person having the conduct of any such waggon or other carriage, shall permit or suffer the Horses drawing the same, whether the same shall be loaded or not, to travel faster than a walk; and that every person offending against this Rule or Order shall, for every such offence, forfeit and pay to the said Company any sum not exceeding ten shillings, nor less than five shillings.

Extracted from the Minute Book of the Company of Proprietors of the Kilmarnock and Troon Railway, and Certified by

JAMES GREGG, Clerk of the Company.

KILMARNOCK, PRINTED BY H. CRAWFORD.

The introduction of the steam locomotive worked its own revolution on the railways. Trials began in Scotland as early as 1817 on the Kilmarnock and Troon Railway. In the central industrial belt a steam locomotive, built for the Monkland and Kirkintilloch Railway Company, first appeared on the rails as a working engine in 1831. Other early railway systems included the Edinburgh and Dalkeith Railway (opened in 1831), the Dundee and Newtyle (incorporated in 1826), the Garnkirk and Glasgow (opened in 1832) and the Edinburgh and Glasgow (incorporated in 1838) which linked the administrative and commercial hearts of Scotland.

In their Report to the Subscribers to the Edinburgh and Glasgow Railway in 1831, Thomas Grainger and John Miller, civil engineers, Edinburgh, extolled the advantages of railway transport over that on the roads and canals:

'Goods carried betwixt Edinburgh, Glasgow, and Leith, it may be premised, are transmitted either by the circuitous route of the Firth of Forth, and Forth and Clyde Canal, or by that Canal and the Union, or by carts and waggons on the public road, at an expense of money, varying from sixteen to forty shillings per ton, and of time, from eighteen hours to four days ... Time is money in all commercial intercourse'. On the railways, they argued: 'While the merchant and manufacturer save in the carriage of their goods, the householder gets cheap coals, the professional man and tourist a cheap and speedy means of conveyance, and the landholder finds an extensive market for his mineral and agricultural produce'.
(Collection of Messrs Hill and Robb: GD.234 Box 3)

2
Illustration of a steam locomotive and train for the Edinburgh and Glasgow Railway, from the 1831 Report. The railway was amalgamated with the North British Railway Company in 1865. (Collection of Messrs Hill and Robb: GD.234 Box 3)

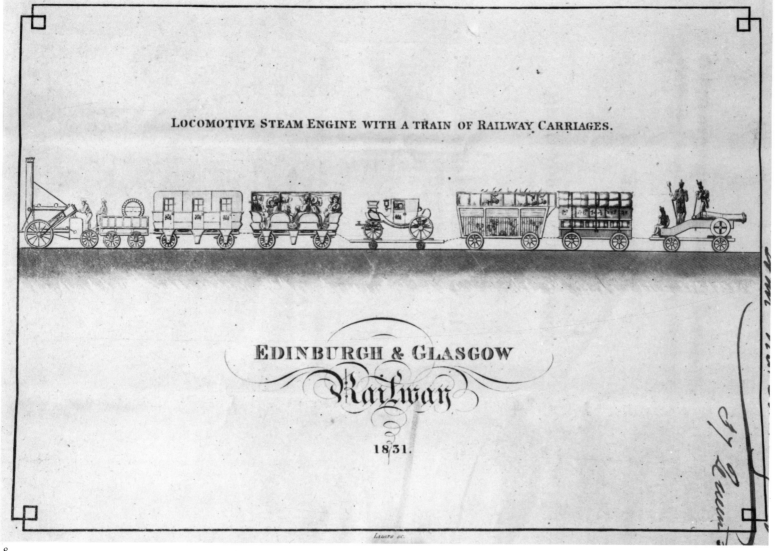

LOCOMOTIVE STEAM ENGINE WITH A TRAIN OF RAILWAY CARRIAGES.

EDINBURGH & GLASGOW
Railway
1831.

3
Drawings of early Scottish steam
locomotives are rare. This diagram of a
locomotive for the Dundee and Newtyle
Railway comes from Justiciary Court
papers relating to an accident, 1836. The
Dundee and Newtyle Railway was
incorporated in 1826 and opened in 1831.
It was later leased to the Caledonian
Railway Company and absorbed into the
London Midland and Scottish Railway in
1923. (Register House Plans: 42535)

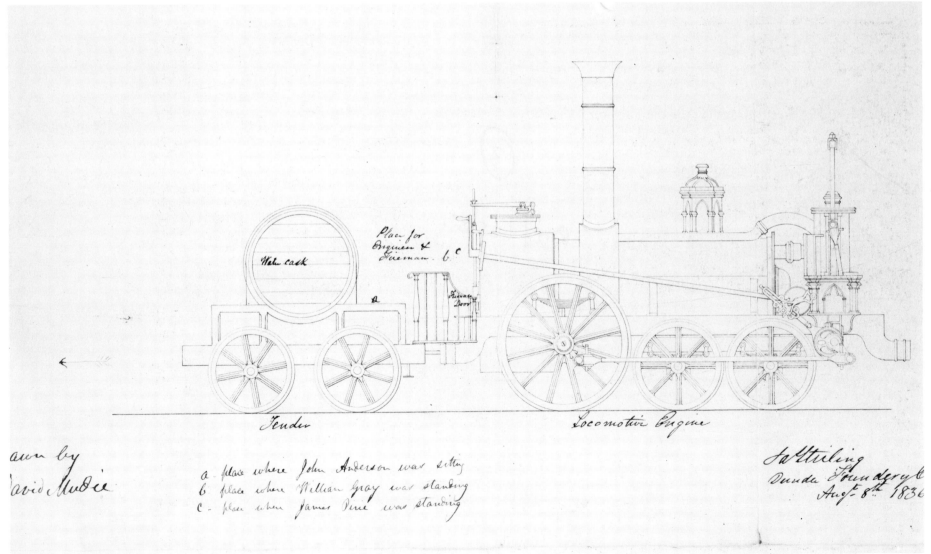

The building of the railways required armies of labourers. Laying the lines, particularly on Scotland's northern scenic routes, was back-breaking work as well as a challenge to engineers and their machinery. Large concentrations of workmen sometimes led to quarrels and disturbances among rival groups and to a concern among officials and public figures for some kind of social and spiritual oversight of the workers.

4

In July 1841 the sheriff of Linlithgowshire reported on 'tumultuous proceedings' among the labourers on the Edinburgh and Glasgow Railway. Although the trouble began simply over a subscription for a gift to one of the Company officials, it was not long before several hundred Highland and Irish workmen were seen marching along the line towards a confrontation. The procurator fiscal at one point read the Riot Act:

> *'... the leaders of the Scotch band had been induced ... to halt within sight of a high Spoil Bank at Priestinch, on which the Irish to the number of 300 or 400 had assembled; armed with bludgeons, scythes, and bayonets on sticks, reaping hooks, iron rods, etc ... a large band of the Irish from Priestinch had passed westwards through Linlithgow between 8 and 9 in the evening with the intention of licking the Scotchmen. They had obliged many men working on the line to accompany them. In passing through Linlithgow 470 were counted.'*

Troops arrived on the fourth day of the dispute. The sheriff ended his Report:

> *'I consider that it is highly desirable that a large number of Railway Policemen should be stationed at the different great works and that at short distances along the line, there should be placed men with horses capable of conveying very early intelligence of any expected outbreak or movement among the labourers'.*

(Lord Advocate's Department: AD.58/66)

5

In a letter to David Rankine of the Caledonian Railway Company in 1846, Charles Stewart of Hillside, factor on the Annandale estates, recommended the services of a schoolmaster and a chaplain to the railway labourers on Evan Water and southwards towards Lockerbie on the construction of the Caledonian Railway:

> *'For the 300 or 400 stationed at Lockerbie, being chiefly Roman Catholic Irish, it was considered best to offer education by the parish schoolmaster. It was thought that by inducing them to spend the evenings otherwise than in dissipation might tend to make them work more steadily and prevent riots. I engaged the parish teacher and usher for this purpose to devote two hours every evening. The men took it in a grateful spirit and from 80 to 100 have been at school regularly for 3 months making great progress in writing and arithmetic ... The clergyman's chief avocation will be among the huts on Evan Water where there are or soon will be upwards of 1,000 of the rudest class of English navvies ... But south of there and in the Lockerbie district, there will generally be 1,000 more who never appear at any place of worship.'*

(BR/CAL/4/74/3)

Even in an age of engineering marvels the Forth Railway Bridge became one of the modern wonders of the world. By the later 19th century there was an urgent need for a bridge at this historic crossing place, due to both the volume of commercial traffic and the number of travellers who were anxious to get to the north of Scotland as quickly as possible. The Firths of Forth and Tay were twin obstacles on the North British Railway Company's route from Edinburgh to Dundee. Publicity for a Bridge claimed that it would knock 26 miles off the journey between these two places then taken by the NBR's rival the Caledonian Railway.

The contract for the bridge was given to a Glasgow firm headed by William Arrol; the engineers were John Fowler and Benjamin Baker. The bridge itself and the approach lines were built by an independent company, the Forth Bridge Railway Company, incorporated for that purpose in 1873; the Company was a joint undertaking of the North British, North Eastern, Midland and Great Northern Railways. Building began in January 1883. By an Act of 1882 the North British Railway Company was to work and maintain the line in perpetuity.

Since its opening on 4 March 1890 the Forth Railway Bridge has been an internationally famous symbol of Scotland and of Victorian engineering achievement.

6
Building the Forth Railway Bridge.
Workmen on viaduct pier number 7
(BR/FOR/4/34/334)

Laying the railway lines and constructing the numerous tunnels, embankments, bridges and viaducts must be counted among the greatest engineering triumphs of the 19th century. It gave opportunity to use both traditional materials, such as stone and iron, and new material, such as steel. The mile upon mile of track often laid through difficult Scottish terrain, with the necessary railway buildings in town and country, are worthy of our admiration in their own right. What is sometimes undervalued is the way in which these great public undertakings, after initial local upheaval had subsided, merged with the landscape in some of the most scenic parts of Scotland.

CUTTING THE FIRST SOD WEST HIGHLAND RAILWAY
402 J B

7
Cutting the first sod, 23 October 1889, for the West Highland Railway. The ceremony was performed by Lord Abinger whose land in Lochaber was crossed by the line of the railway. The West Highlands were among the scenic routes enjoyed by many travellers for the first time, from the comfort of a railway carriage. (BR/WEH/4/3)

8
Steam navvy at work at Achendaul on the West Highland Railway; the builders had to blast their way through solid rock. (BR/WEH/4/3)

Many city suburbs sprang up and outlying small villages grew into towns as the railways made it possible to commute to town for work, business and pleasure. The railway companies offered inducements, such as cheap travel, to those building houses along the railway lines. Holiday resorts developed as the railways took travellers up into the Highlands and west coast.

9
Strathpeffer, Easter Ross, which owed its popularity as a holiday resort to its mineral springs and its development to the Highland Railway. (BR/GEN(S)/3/122)

10

Notice offering free railway travel to persons building villas within a mile of any of the stations on the Edinburgh and Glasgow Railway, undated. (BR/EGR/4/15)

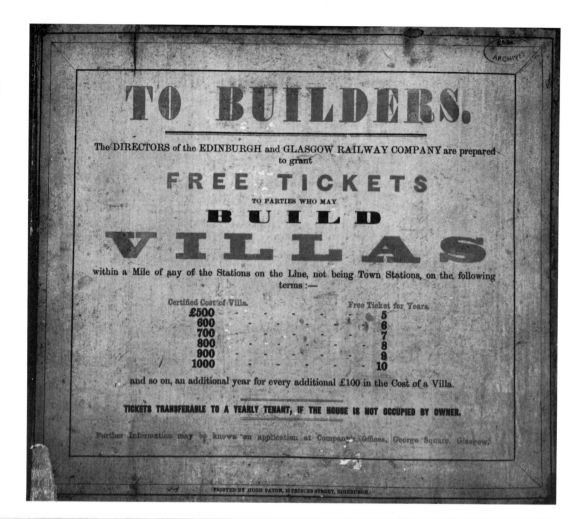

11

Colinton Station in the early 20th century, when the village was still on the outskirts of Edinburgh. (from Views of Juniper Green and District, *1912; collection of Mrs J Tweedie. Reproduced by permission of the Royal Commission on the Ancient and Historical Monuments of Scotland.)*

While many communities welcomed and even petitioned for the establishment of a railway station in their locality there were others who objected to some of the changes which the railway brought in its wake, such as Sunday travel or the 'desecration' and pollution of townscape or countryside. As early as the 1830s, when so many Scottish companies were formed, many people urged moderation on the railway planners.

Various sections of the community saw the coming of the railways as a threat: the coach proprietors understandably regarded the railways as the latter were to regard the motor car nearly a century later; landed proprietors, while many benefited financially from selling land to the companies, were not always certain that their rights were sufficiently protected in these deals.

12
Part of a petition to the Greenock and Ayrshire Railway Company from farmers and others in Kilmacolm parish for a station at Port Glasgow, 1869.
(BR/GAR/7/2)

13

Part of a petition to the Glasgow and South Western Railway Company by local people objecting to golf at Turnberry on Sundays, attendances being facilitated by the Company's Sunday service, [between 1908 and 1916]. (BR/GSW/4/80)

14

Photograph of a Ladies' Golf Tournament at Turnberry, 1912. (Matthew of Gourdiehill Muniments: GD.316/214)

Petition
to the Directors of the Glasgow & South Western Railway Company
against
Sunday Golf at Turnberry.

We, the undersigned, being permanent dwellers (above the age of 21 years) in the district most contiguous to Turnberry Golf Course, desire to make known to the Directors of the Glasgow & South Western Railway Company our strong conviction that the practice recently introduced of playing golf over the said course on Sundays is not only contrary to the traditions of the parish, but a grave encroachment upon the seemliness and sacredness of the Lord's Day, and calculated to do injury to the cause of religion. We rejoiced when, last April, notices were posted up by the authority of the directors declaring that the Golf Course and Club House were closed on Sundays; and we now think it right to call the attention of the directors to the fact that their notices are being systematically disregarded; and to urge upon them the necessity of ensuring that they are strictly adhered to.

James Campbell

Barbara Campbell

D. McCulloch

M. McCulloch

Robert Ferguson

A. R. Ferguson

Jane Newcastle Sanderson

Isabella Sloan

Barbara Sloan

Margaret Andrew

Hugh Rodger

Mrs Hugh Rodger

Mrs Andrew McBrindle

Mary McBrindle

Mrs John Murray

Mrs Hugh Boden

Mr Hugh Boden

Bella Sloan

John McClure sen

John McClure son

Thomas Girvan

Jane Girvan

Sketch of what the 'valley' between the Old and New Towns of Edinburgh might have looked like had the railway not come through the centre of the city. From a pamphlet entitled 'The Great Railway Question', drawn from angry letters to the papers from those who deplored the effects of what the rival railway companies (Caledonian and North British) had done to the centre of the capital city, 1890.

'When Railways get an Inch, they often take an ell;

Where they find a heaven, they often leave a hell'.

'In judging Railway Schemes, keep ONE eye on the present, and A HUNDRED on the future'.
(Collection of Dundas and Wilson, CS: GD.282/13/262)

£100 REWARD.

WHEREAS, on the Night of Saturday the 11th September, instant, some maliciously disposed Person or Persons did lay a TREE across the Rails of the

CALEDONIAN RAILWAY

on the ESK VIADUCT, by which, had it not been perceived in time, the most frightful consequences to the Ten P.M. Train must have ensued.

The Directors of the Caledonian Railway Company hereby offer a Reward of £100 for such information as will lead to the conviction of the offender or offenders within Three Months from this date.

By Order,
J. W. CODDINGTON,
Secretary.

EDINBURGH, 14th September 1847.

PETER BROWN, PRINTER, EDINBURGH.

16
Caledonian Railway Company notice offering a reward of £100 for information on an act of vandalism on the line at the Esk Viaduct, 1847. The incident, which took place only one day after the line opened, may have been sabotage by the anti-railway lobby. (BR/CAL/4/7)

PART 2:

The companies' servants

*t*he railways brought into being a vast range of new employments, manual, administrative and clerical. Thousands of the companies' servants were photographed over the generations beside the engines which symbolised the power and excitement of the transport revolution.

17
A group of employees of the Glasgow and Paisley Joint Line Committee photographed with 0-4-0T locomotive No 1; a note on the back of the photograph records that this was the first engine to be built at Paisley Greenlaw, [undated, 19th century]. (BR/GPJ/5/1)

Designs for locomotives and rolling stock were brought to life in the workshops of the railway companies, where the working trains were also repaired. A stream of apprentices joined the army of craftsmen in forge and smithy, machine shops, wheel and axle sections, erecting shops, boiler shops and brass and iron foundries.

18
Employees of the London and North Eastern Railway in the Company's boiler shop at the Inverurie Works in 1929. (BR/GNS/4/47/15)

19
Part of a roll of apprentices at the Caledonian Railway Company's St Rollox Works, Glasgow, 1895-1920. (BR/CAL/15/13)

LIST OF SPECIAL APPRENTICES.

Name.	Apprenticeship commenced on	expires on	Drawing Office Entered	Left	REMARKS.
Robert Hindmarch.	April 1900.	April 1905.	20th Feb. 1905.	29 APRIL 1905	
Austine Thomson,	15th Jany. 1900.	14th Jany. 1905.	22nd Dec. 1904.	29 APRIL 1905	Son of Wagon Painter.
Kenneth Sclater,	26th March 1900.	25th March 1905.			
John Watts,	11th Jany. 1899.	31st March 1905.			
Albert Conner,	17th April 1900.	16th April 1905.	1 MAY 1905	14 July 1905	Mr. Barr of Glenfield & Kennedy, Kilmarnock, per Mr. Urie.
Leslie Walters,	1st Augt. 1900.	31st July, 1905.	1 MAY 1905	30 June 1905	Mr. Brand, G. M. Office.
James Gibson,	1st Augt. 1900.	31st July, 1905.	1 MAY 1905	30 June 1905	Mr. John Strain.
Esmond Keelan,	2nd Augt. 1900.	1st Augt. 1905.	1 Aug 1905	22 Sept 1905	D.W.Campbell, v late of India.
David Suter,	13th Augt. 1900.	12th Augt. 1905.	3 July 1905	28	
Harold Henderson,	18th Sept. 1900.	17th Sept. 1905.	3 July 1905	16 Sept 1905	Marquis of Breadalbane.
Wm. Steel,	22nd Octr. 1900.	21st Octr. 1905.	20 Aug 1905	30 Decr 1905	Per R. J. Patrick.
Thos. S. Brown,	5th Novr. 1900.	4th Novr. 1905.	18 Sept 1905	11 Decr 1905	Mr. Urie.
Robert Richardson,	14th Jany. 1901.	13th Jany. 1906.	2 Oct 1905	30 Decr 1905	Son of Driver, Stirling.
John Rodgerson,	26th Feby. 1901.	25th Feby. 1906.	12 Decr 1905	24 Feby 1906	Mr. Urie.
Henry Heinig,	6th March 1901.	5th March 1906.	11 Jany 1906	31 march 1906	D.W.Campbell, late of India, - P10/789.
James Watson,	29th April 1901.	28th April 1906.	9 Jany 1906	28 April 1906	Son of late James Watson, Foreman Boilermaker.
Wm. Harrower,	28th May, 1901.	27th May, 1906.	26 Feby 1906	26 May 1906	Son of Mr. Harrower, Bowling.
Wm. Duncan,	21st Augt. 1901.	20th Augt. 1906.	10 Sept 1906	3 Novr 1906	Son of Mr. Duncan, Rector of Annan Academy.
Symon Ayton,	5th Augt. 1901.	4th Augt. 1906.	Does not wish into Drawing office.		
John Allison,	19th Augt. 1901.	18th Augt. 1906.	2 April 1906	1 Sep 1906	
Andrew Fleming,	26th Augt. 1901.	25th Augt. 1906.	28 May 1906	1 Sep 1906	Insp. Fleming, Polmadie.
Arch. Scott,	3rd Octr. 1901.	2nd Octr. 1906.	30 April 1906	1 Sep 1906	Dr. McDonald.
H. B. Little,	10th Feby. 1902.	9th Feby. 1907.	3 Sept 1906	1 Sep 1906	Father in Canal House, Port Dundas.
John Ruthven,	1st April 1902.	31st March 1907.	Left Service		Son of Mr. Ruthven, G.M.Office
James Burden,	27th April 1902.	26th April 1907.	3 Sep 1906	2 march 1907	Mr. Samuel, Stirling.
John Croxford,	4th Augt. 1902.	3rd Augt. 1907.	Does not wish to go to D.Office		Recommended by Mr. Millhouse.
John Reekie,	18th Augt. 1902.	17th Augt. 1907.	Left service		Mr. Reekie, Ardgaith, Nithsdale Rd, Dumbreck, P2/1002
Norman D. Shove	2nd Sept. 1902.	1st Sept. 1907.			Recommended by Mr. A. Cunningham
Charles Lorimer,	22nd Sept. 1902.	21st Sept. 1907.			The Limes, Belmont Park, Lee, S E

In addition to practical staff training and experience gained on the job many railwaymen belonged to local Mutual Improvement Classes. These groups, which met to hear lectures on and discuss the skills of their trade, also provided a means of social contact and helped to maintain the feelings of brotherhood and community that existed among the workforce.

20
Footplate staff of St Margaret's (later Edinburgh District) Railwaymen's Mutual Improvement Class with LNER Class J37 0-6-0 locomotive No 9488; photographed between 1929 and 1939. Third figure from the right (in cap) is John Mackenzie who throughout his railway career was a leader of the Improvement Class and its activities. (Miscellaneous Collections: GD.1/908/9)

21
British Railways Mutual Improvement Class, Muirkirk Shed, Ayrshire, undated. (D L Smith Collection: GD.422/18/115)

22

Caledonian Railway Company: pages
from Rules and Regulations,
Superintendent's Standing Orders:
Engineer's Instructions to Inspectors
of Way and Works, *1868.*
(BR/RB(S)/1/2)

14. Whenever part of a train is left upon the **Main Line** from accident, or inability of the engine to bring the whole forward, the Engineman must not return for it on the same line, except by written instructions from the Guard, but must go on to the proper line and cross at the nearest points behind the part left, which he must push before him till convenient to go in front again with the engine.

15. If, in case of accident, an engine is unavoidably obliged to pass for a short distance on a wrong line, the Guard or Fireman must go or send some other competent person back to the next Signalman, and obtain his permission in writing for the engine to run on the WRONG LINE to his post, and the Engineman must not, under any circumstances, move in the wrong direction until such permission has been obtained in writing, and he must not proceed further than the nearest cross-over road, when the engine must be turned on the proper line of rails.

16. Danger whistles will be given by the deep-toned whistle in cases where the engine is supplied with two whistles, or where no such provision exists, by three or more sharp, short, quick whistles by the ordinary engine whistle. Immediately upon hearing such signals, the Guard must apply his break.

17. No person is to be allowed to ride on the engine or in the Guard's break without a special written order from one of the principal officers of the Company owning the train, authorising him to do so.

18. Guards and Enginemen must report at the first Station at which they stop, any defect they may have observed in the signals, works, permanent

way or telegraph, and also report the same in their journals.

19. The movements of the train are under the direction of the Guard, to whose instructions as to stopping starting, &c., the Engineman must pay implicit attention.

REGULATIONS AS TO GUARDS.

20. Each Passenger Guard must, when on duty, have with him his watch, and must take with him in his van, a Red, a Green, and a White Flag, a box of Detonating Signals (not less than 12), a Hand Signal Lamp, a Whistle, two or more spare Couplings, and one tail signal board to be used to indicate " SPECIAL FOLLOWING;" in addition to the above, each Goods and Mineral Guard shall carry a box of Grease, with Knife and Probe, a Tow-rope, and a couple of Sprags.

21. Every Guard should be in attendance at the station from which he is to start half-an-hour before the time appointed for departure, and must satisfy himself before starting that the train is properly marshalled, coupled, lamped, greased, that the breaks are in good working order, and that the train is in all respects in a state of efficiency for travelling.

22. When trains are shunted for other trains to pass, the tail lamps must be removed, or so disposed as not to exhibit the red light to the following train.

23. When from any cause a train is unable to proceed at a greater speed than **four** miles an hour the Guard, if there be one, or the Rear-Guard if there be

Women employed in the railway workshops during the First World War: above, cleaning a locomotive; below, in the workshop. (From Women's War Work, issued by the War Office in September 1916: BR/LIB(S)/10/21)

SIGNALBOX REPORT.
D.O. ....

Station Master. Mr. McWhirter.

Name of Signalbox ...CAMBUS...........

Date of visit.   1st March, 1945.

Name of Woman.   Mrs. Eliz. Hamilton.

Grade.   5th Grade.

Domestic circumstances.   Mrs. Hamilton has no children.   Her
                          husband is missing since the fall of Singapore.

Exact location of Box.   About 25 yards from Station.

Nearest inhabited house.   Surrounded by houses.

Telephone Communication.   Between Cambus Junction Signalbox and
                           cabin.
Hours of duty.   7am. to 6 pm.
                           2pm. to 10pm.
                           10pm. to 7 am.

Hours of duty of
  Station staff.   7am. to 10pm.

Type of Portering involved.   Light portering duties.

Lamp Duties.

Whether operates
  Crossing Gates.   Yes.

Sanitary and Washing
  arrangements.   None.   Use of lavatory facilities at station,
                         but this is most inconvenient, as every time
          the signalwoman wishes to make use of the station facilities, she
          has to telephone the signalman at Cambus Junction to see if the l
Type of Water Supply.   line is clear as it is impossible to hear the
                         bell in the signalbox from the ladies' waiting
                         room.

Drainage.

Cooking and heating.   Coal fire.

Lighting.   Gas.

Distance to cycle or walk
  home.   5 minutes' walk.

Woman's reaction to job.   She likes her job very much and finds it
                         most interesting.

REMARKS.   Mrs. Hamilton finds no difficulty with the operation of the
  signal levers.
           I would suggest that a flush lavatory be provided at this
  signalbox.   The structure for this might be erected at the foot of
  the stairs leading to the signalbox, and I would also suggest that
  a wash-hand basin with running water be installed in the signalbox.
  As an alternative I recommend that an "Elsan" closet be provided and
  a wash-hand basin and pedestal.

25
London and North Eastern Railway: page from a file relating to the employment of women at signalboxes during the Second World War, c.1944-5. (BR/LNE/8/382)

The running of the railways required an army of 'white-collar' employees, who were photographed almost as often as the men who worked on the railways themselves.

26
The Goods Manager and office staff of the Glasgow and South Western Railway Company, 1894. (D L Smith Collection: GD.422/18/108)

NORTH BRITISH RAILWAY.

Memorial from the Clerical Staff re Increased Cost of Living. 1916.

SIGNATURE.	DESIGNATION.	STATION.
Jns. Redpath	Booking Clerk	Perth
John Wallace	Telegraph Clerk	do.
Leslie Fairfoul	Clerk (Booking)	Luthrie
David Stark	Clerk	Lindores
James Clark	Telegraph Clerk	Perth
John Taber	Clerk (Booking)	Milnathort
George Kirk	Goods Clerk	Lochleven
Patrick Clark	Booking Clerk	Loch Leven
William Emslie	Booking Clerk	Kinross Junction
David Braid	Goods Clerk	Kinross Junction
Charles Watters	Goods Clerk	Milnathort
Charles M. Whyte	Relief Clerk	Cossie
Jas. F. Morris	Goods Clerk	Newburgh
Dora Batterson	Goods Clerkess	Do.
Lav. Goodwillie	Clerk (Spare)	Do.
Tom Sutherland	Clerk	Abernethy
Wm. Melville	Parcel Clerk	Perth
James Morton	Parcel Clerk	Perth
Lewis Waddell	Parcel Clerk	Perth

27

Memorial from the clerical staff of the North British Railway Company about salaries and the increased cost of living during the First World War, 1916. The volume from which it comes contains the signatures of many staff from stations along the NBR line. (BR/NBR/7/3)

28

National Union of Railwaymen: details of rates of pay of locomotive running staff, drivers, firemen and cleaners, 1927. (BR/LAS(S)/40)

Authority	RATES OF PAY—DRIVERS (SECTION 1).	
	Train Drivers and Shed Enginemen with continuous footplate service who were engaged on shed duties on August 18th, 1919.	
1937	First and second years .... 12s. per day.	
	Third and fourth years .... 13s. per day.	
	Fifth year .... 14s. per day.	
	Sixth year....................... 15s. per day.	

DEFINITION OF SHED ENGINEMEN ENTITLED TO RECEIVE ABOVE RATES (CATEGORY "A.")

Appx. "C" — Shed enginemen who, on August 18th, 1919, were engaged on the duties of shed relieving, turning, stabling, and preparing engines, etc., and who have continuous footplate service, are entitled to advance to the maximum servitude rate.

DRIVERS TRANSFERRED FROM TRAIN TO SHUNTING WORK OWING TO FAILING EYESIGHT.

N.W.B.—22/12/24 — Drivers who are reduced from train work to shunting work on account of failing eyesight are entitled to retain the rate of pay they were receiving for train work.

DRIVERS TRANSFERRED FROM TRAIN WORK TO SHUNTING DUTIES AT OWN REQUEST.

N.W.B.—22/12/1924 — Drivers transferred to shunting work at their own request are only entitled to receive the rate laid down for this class of work, i.e., a maximum of 14s. per day.

DRIVERS TRANSFERRED FROM TRAIN TO SHUNTING WORK AT DISCRETION OF COMPANY.

N.W.B.—18/12/1923 — Drivers put on shunting work to suit the convenience of the company are entitled to retain their servitude rate for such work.

5

SHED ENGINEMEN, CATEGORY "D," AND LIABILITY TO SUPERSESSION.

Agreement of 28/7 1920 — Men in Category "D" are liable to be taken off their duties as shed enginemen in the event of a man with continuous footplate service having to be taken off his own work in consequence of physical disability or failing eyesight.

SHED ENGINEMEN AND SLIDING SCALE.

2nd Memo. — Shed enginemen, including those who fall within Category "D," are entitled to receive any sliding scale payments that may fall due to locomotivemen in the ordinary line of promotion.

RATE OF PAY OF FIREMEN (SECTION 3).

All Firemen Except Those Shed Firemen Coming Under Section 4.

1937	First and second years...... 9s. 6d. per day.
	Third and fourth years . 10s. 6d. per day.
	Fifth until completion of tenth year................. 11s. per day (max.)
	After ten years firing...... 12s. per day.
	(If not appointed as driver)

ELIGIBILITY FOR MINIMUM DRIVING RATE AFTER TEN YEARS FIRING.

1937 — Firemen who have completed ten years' service as such, including turns of firing worked prior to appointment as firemen, are entitled to receive the minimum driving rate.

FIREMEN WHO HAVE WORKED 313 DRIVING SHIFTS AND NOT APPOINTED AS DRIVERS.

1937 — Firemen who have worked 313 driving shifts, but who have not completed ten years' firing service, are entitled to receive the maximum firing rate for any firing work performed.

8

Like many other trade unions that of the railwaymen emerged from earlier Friendly Societies of railway company employees in the 1850s. Various local unions were eventually united in 1871 in the Amalgamated Society of Railway Servants, founded 'to promote a good and fair understanding between employers and employed', although the Scottish Society of Railway Servants resisted amalgamation until 1892. In 1913 many remaining local unions were absorbed in the National Union of Railwaymen.

NORTH BRITISH, GLASGOW & SOUTH-WESTERN, AND CALEDONIAN RAILWAYS.

12th July, 1866.

UNION OF RAILWAY SERVANTS.

It having been reported to the Directors of the several Railway Companies in Scotland that certain meetings have been held, and that others are in contemplation, for the expressed purpose of **"the attainment of our** (Railway Servants) **rights,"** &c.

The Directors hereby give notice to the **"Engine-Drivers, Firemen, Passenger and Goods Guards, Passenger and Goods Porters and Pointsmen,"** that while they with their several Officers are most desirous of meeting the legitimate demands of their Employees, they will most firmly withstand all dictation by the men; and they give notice that any attempt at combination by the respective Employees will be met by the Directors in such a manner as may to them seem fit.

The Directors take this opportunity of cautioning those in their employ against combination, or joining any union for the avowed purpose of dictating to their Employers.

THOS. K. ROWBOTHAM, GENERAL MANAGER,
North British Railway Co.

W. JOHNSTONE, GENERAL MANAGER,
Glasgow and South-Western Railway Co.

C. JOHNSTONE, GENERAL MANAGER,
Caledonian Railway Co.

29
Reply of the Directors of the North British, Glasgow and South Western and Caledonian Railway Companies to their employees' demand for a meeting, forbidding the latter to make 'any attempt at combination', 12 July 1866.
(BR/LIB(S)/6/224)

In November 1889 a demand was made to the companies for a 10-hour day, overtime pay, annual holidays and a guaranteed week's work. When the companies declined arbitration, in October-November 1890, 8500 men came out on strike paralysing traffic and stopping public works. Evictions from company housing provoked disturbances. There was further industrial action in 1891. Fears of unemployment among railwaymen were realised as a result of the absorption of the Scottish railways into the two lines of the London and North Eastern and the London Midland and Scottish in 1923. Railwaymen gave solid backing to the General Strike of 1926 in support of the miners.

30
The Great Railway Strike: *a pamphlet calling for lessons in industrial relations to be learned from the 1891 strike.*
(BR/LIB(S)/6/224/342)

4

THE GREAT RAILWAY STRIKE.

THE strike of railway servants over Scotland calls for very serious consideration. It has been protracted, and has so deeply affected the whole community, that many lessons, comparatively lost to view in other trade disputes, have been pushed into public notice in this case. As all classes are deeply interested in the labour questions of the day, it is desirable that attention be given to any case whose details have become very generally known.

Fortunately, we can now reason out the matter without coming into collision with the angry passions which have been roused to a white heat. During the struggle, the war-spirit and the war-path settled everything. Every man who opened his lips or took up his pen on the subject was either for the men or against them,—for the railway companies or against them. Now, we may discuss the subject more deliberately, and with less offence to those most deeply concerned. A quieter time may give us opportunity for noting the light that has been thrown on some of the thorny questions involved in all our trade disputes. We believe that if a real lasting good to the community is to come out of this strike, the case of both parties must be put in the strongest possible form, and each party in the struggle must consider the opposite case in its best light. This may be impossible while the fight is proceeding; but it is both possible and wise after the conflict is over. Our wish is to attempt a full and fair representation of the conflicting interests. The want of intimate knowledge of the service may prove a serious disadvantage to us, but our readers—specially the railway workers among them—will make liberal allowance for this.

The interests affected by the conflict are vast. A highly-respected body of public servants have their life-interests deeply involved; the great companies, which are concerned in meeting the general requirements of the country, have had their stability threatened; the whole community have found their travelling facilities, even though provided under Act of Parliament, suddenly curtailed, and in many instances terminated. It is impossible to exaggerate the importance of a conflict so serious.

The lessons of the struggle so depend on its history that the main facts need to be stated. For a considerable time—certainly for more than a year—complaints from railway servants, on account of long hours of work, found general and reiterated expression; these complaints were formally presented to officials and directors of the several railway companies. The servants were not left without assurances that their complaints would have consideration; nor were they denied some concessions; but it is alleged that nothing practical was done, and that the men were left to toil on with no prospect

of such relief as they considered fairly due. They further allege, that in some cases men who pressed on the attention of the leading officers of the companies the general claims were, on this account, dismissed the service soon afterwards. These allegations, if correct, present not only reasonable, but strong grounds of complaint. The companies allege that they have met the men in a fair spirit, and have done much to improve their condition. An important modification of the charge against them has been made at the instance of the directors of one of the companies by re-publication of a circular of 19th November last, shewing that complaints first submitted by the men in December previous had been considered, and that a committee had been appointed to meet with 'any deputation of employees of the various departments;' and this procedure resulted in lighter work, or a raised scale of wages. In this way several items of information have come out. As to work in the signal-boxes, for example, the statement runs thus,—'A large number of our signal-men work eight hours per day, a number ten hours per day, and we have not one whose hours exceed twelve per day.' As to extras in pay, it is stated that 'premiums, ranging from £3 to £5 per annum, are allowed to each man not concerned in any casualty during any twelve months.' It is satisfactory to the public, as indicating the safety of railway travelling under ordinary conditions, to learn that this 'involves an expenditure by the company of £12,000 a-year.' Long may this reasonable reward for regard to public safety and to the condition of rolling stock continue to stand at this figure, or vary only by exceeding it. These statements, illustrative of what has been going on, seem to shew that a considerable degree of improvement in the service has been gained by quiet agitation during 1890.

But such gains seemed to the men small in comparison with what they desired. They presented a rather lengthened series of demands, into the details of which it is not now needful to enter, as these became concentrated at length in the threefold claim for a ten-hours' working day, time-and-a-quarter pay for overtime, and time-and-a-half for Sunday labour. The dispute came to its height over this. The demand was an ultimatum from the men, deliberately refused by the companies. This brought on the fight. The men began preparations for a strike, and the companies had full warning that preparations were being made for conflict. It took place just before Christmas. The object was to take the companies at a time when the difficulties of the fight would be greatest for them, and when the paralysing of the trade of the country would be most serious. Regarded as 'fighting tactics,' the plan was skilful, with this serious drawback, to which railway workers are constantly exposed, that the difficulties of the companies cannot be thus increased without widespread irritation over the country, and loss of sympathy for the strikers.

The consequences are now well known, and we wish to look the lessons fairly in the face. They are quite marked for all concerned,—men, companies, and the public. As the men took the responsibility of declaring war, it seems specially important that

32

Extract from 'The Railmen's Bulletin' during the 1926 General Strike:

The first position that confronted the committee was the steps that should be taken to ensure that all our members would leave off duty at their home stations by 6 am on the morning of the strike, and ... that all men should take steps to reach home by 5 am. Unfortunately things did not work out according to plans, and the Committee had to take steps to send men home to Fort William, Aberdeen, Dundee, Greenock, Berwick, Dumfries, Carlisle and London. Some of our members were also stranded at Aberdeen, Perth and Dundee and steps were taken to bring them home to Glasgow ...

Irvine reports that Harbour, station and works are closed.

Ayr, famed for honest men and bonnie lassies, has also established a 'strike reputation'. This reputation is being maintained and added to through the solid front being presented by our ASLEF and NUR comrades.

Kirkintilloch is generally looked upon as a mere country village; nevertheless in a dispute of this description it is bound to have an important say in the successful application of our policy ... to prevent the movement of goods by road and rail. Kirkintilloch interpret this to mean that all motor buses are due to be held up as well as trains.

During the miners' lockout of 1921 our Barrhead branch played a prominent part in preventing the movement of coal. In this bit of trouble they are keeping our members solid from the 'Shaws' to Stewarton.

Coatbridge, Hamilton, Airdrie, Burnbank and Motherwell are all vital railway centres. Joint strike committees of all unions interested in the welfare of our 'shock troops' have been set up, and the position is as solid as either iron or steel could make it. A report was received from our Motherwell Committee that 22 members of the Blacksmiths Union remained at their work. We raised the position with the local official in Glasgow and the men were instructed to cease work.
(A G Dunbar Collection: GD.344/6/70)

31

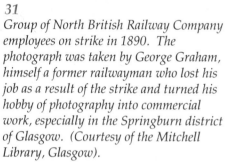

Group of North British Railway Company employees on strike in 1890. The photograph was taken by George Graham, himself a former railwayman who lost his job as a result of the strike and turned his hobby of photography into commercial work, especially in the Springburn district of Glasgow. (Courtesy of the Mitchell Library, Glasgow).

33
London and North Eastern Railway:
Inverurie Locomotive Works Fire Brigade,
undated (BR/LNE/15/92/1)

34
London Midland and Scottish
Railway staff safety manual, 1924.
(BR/RB(S)/2/107)

IS IT SAFE

TO walk or stand foul of the four-foot if it can be avoided?

Look where you're going!—A Man who stepped foul of a running line forgot this advice. He was caught by a Light Engine and killed.

REMEMBER! "**Prevention is better than Cure.**"

10

IS IT SAFE

TO touch the electric rails—unless you are properly protected (see page 47)?

TO work capstans or interfere with them in any way unless you are authorised to do so?

TO manipulate Electric platform trucks unless you are a properly trained and authorised driver?

TO stand so near the rails that you may get knocked down by a passing train or vehicle?

TO walk along the line except when it is necessary in the execution of your duty? (Should you be obliged to do so, always face the traffic; **even then keep a good look-out, as "single line" working may be in operation.** Take special precaution when walking along a single line.).

REMEMBER! "**Prevention is better than Cure.**"

11

RULES.

I.

THAT this Society shall be called the CALEDONIAN Name.
RAILWAY SERVANTS' FRIENDLY SOCIETY.

II

That this Society shall be constituted of an unlimited Constitution.
number of honorary and ordinary Members.

III.

Every person contributing by benefaction twenty Honorary Members.
shillings and upwards, or by an annual subscription
not less than ten shillings, shall become an honorary
Member, but not so as to be entitled by any such benefaction or subscription, to any benefit or emolument
from the funds of this Society.

IV.

The ordinary Members of this Society shall consist Ordinary Members.
of males in the employ of the Caledonian Railway Co.,
who, at the time of admission, shall be in good health,
and shall have attained the age of fifteen years.

PAYMENTS TO BE MADE AND BENEFITS ALLOWED.

The Contributions to be paid by Members, and the Benefits to be allowed by the Society,
shall be according to the undernoted Tables, subject to the reductions and conditions specified
in the following Rules :—

CLASS.	ENTRANCE FEE.	WEEKLY CONTRIBUTION.		WEEKLY SICK ALLOWANCE.	FUNERAL ALLOWANCE.	
					Death of Member.	Death of Member's Wife.
A	1/	3d.	Secures	6/	£4	£2
B	1/6	4½d.	,,	9/	6	3
C	2/	6d.	,,	12/	8	4
D	3/	7½d.	,,	15/	10	5

XIX.   16

NOTE.—Engine-drivers, Firemen, Goods and Mineral Breaksmen must pay one-third
more Entrance Fee and Weekly Contribution than shown in the above Tables, to secure the
same benefits of any class they may join. This is found necessary, to provide for the
extra risk.

W. WOOD, ACTUARY.

Each Member must be furnished with a copy of the Society's Rules, for which he shall pay 2d.

35
*Rules of the Caledonian Railway
Servants' Friendly Society, 1857.
Friendly Societies' welfare functions
continued into the era of the Unions who
were primarily concerned with pay and
working conditions. (BR/WEL(S)/26)*

The Railwayman's Catechism, 1875:
detailing the welfare provisions that came
with membership of The Amalgamated
Society of Railway Servants.
(BR/LAS(S)/76)

THE RAILWAYMAN'S CATECHISM.

Are Societies useful and beneficial to Working Men?

Yes.

Why are they so?

Because by the unity of interests the risk of each is borne by all, thus creating an insurance and security of provision and protection which individually cannot be done.

Which is the best Railwayman's Society?

THE AMALGAMATED SOCIETY OF RAILWAY SERVANTS.

What are its objects?

To provide assistance when out of employment, and give means to seek for work. Superannuation for those who are old or are disabled by accident, and Legal Assistance in obtaining justice and defending our rights.

Has it any other object?

Yes. To secure reasonable hours of duty, and fair payment in return. To reduce Sunday duty. When work is done on the Seventh Day, to obtain payment for it; and to obtain payment in fair proportion for all work done beyond the stipulated day's duration.

What else?

To bring about a good understanding between employers and employed, by advocating what is just to both. To obtain compensation for those who suffer loss by unnecessary accidents, by getting the *Compensation Laws* justly amended, and thus striving to decrease the present fearful slaughter on our lines, and make railway travelling safer. It aims to stop the injustices so often inflicted on Railwaymen by those who hold intermediate offices, and gives to every man independency of spirit, and courage to assert his own rights.

How does it hope to accomplish these objects?

By creating an earnest unity and confidence amongst its members, so that the interest of one becomes that of every one. Unity is a tower of strength to working men, and when supported by available funds can exact respect from powerful and arbitrary companies or employers which they are unwilling to give to individuals when disunited. *Many can help one where one cannot help many.*

Does the Society encourage strikes?

No; it avoids them as an evil to masters and men. But it courts favour from the Public and the Press by acting with moderation, and its members with self-respect. It has moreover shown that the Public are, on their own account, deeply interested in the success of the movement.

How does the Society respect the Companies?

By respecting discipline and the just claims they may make on our labour, and by refusing to lend its aid to those members who wilfully refuse or neglect their duty to their employers. Whilst contending for its members' rights, it seeks no wrong to the Companies.

What are the monetary benefits of the Amalgamated Society?

Ten Shillings per week for ten weeks if out of work from causes not under the member's control; and Five Shillings per week for ten weeks more. Travelling Relief of Ten Shillings per week when seeking employment. Five Shillings per week Superannuation Allowance for life if disabled by accident, or by reason of old age, and Legal Assistance *to any amount* (£100 if necessary) for a just cause in connection with our occupation.

How many members does it contain?

Twenty thousand.

Where can a Railwayman join?

At any of the Two Hundred Branches in England and Wales.

What are the Payments for each Member?

Entrance Two Shillings; contributions Threepence per week, except when over thirty-five years of age, and in consequence of superannuation, it is then Fourpence per week.

What is the best thing a Railwayman can do?

JOIN THE SOCIETY AT ONCE. It secures the advantages already mentioned, makes men more friendly to each other, gives us encouragement to ask our rights, the desire to assist one another in distress, and often helps the widow and little ones when the father is laid low. JOIN AT ONCE! and secure protection against the emergencies of your calling; obtain the friendly brotherly feeling of each other, and the co-operation of your mates throughout the country.

FRED. W. EVANS, *General Secretary.*

25, FINSBURY PLACE, E.C., *September 17, 1875.*

NOTE.—At the close of **1874** there was **£9,300 in hand,** 6,000 New Members gained, and £4,000 was saved during the year. At the close of this year (1875) the Funds in hand will probably exceed £14,000. The Society has been 3½ years in existence.

Living on the job: engineers' living accommodation at Loch Treig during the building of the West Highland Railway, c.1890. (BR/WEH/4/3/35)

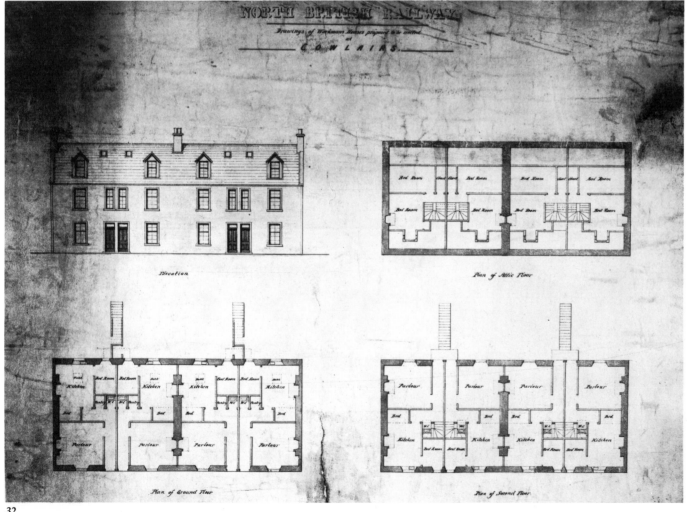

38
Railwaymen and their families often lived in company houses, forming distinctive communities around stations, along the lines and overlooking the locomotive works or other concentrations of railway activity. This drawing shows proposed workmen's housing at Cowlairs, Glasgow, to be built by the North British Railway Company, 1872. (Register House Plans: 16201)

39

British Railways Welcomes You: *a pamphlet for new staff on the nationalised railway network, [1949].*

> *'This British Railways "family" is bound to be strange to you at first. But it really is a family on a big scale ...*
>
> *British Railways have a long tradition of service faithfully performed. We stand high in the esteem of the peoples of this country and of countries overseas. It is good to remember that British pioneers gave railways to the world, and despite the fact that others who followed learned by our mistakes – we suffered the penalties of all pioneers – our industry still holds a premier position among the world's railways. That, you know, is something of which to be proud'.*
> (BR/LIB(S)/15/160)

Those who serve —

ABOVE—*On Railway Ships at Sea.*
BELOW—*In Locomotive Works.*

Training for Efficiency —

Police College.
Works Apprentices' School.
Booking Office Training.

A Signalling School.
A Residential School.
Enquiry Office Training.

Staff 'Faults and Fines Book' of the
Glasgow, Paisley, Kilmarnock and Ayr
Railway Company, 1840-74.
(BR/GPK/4/1)

April 10 John Johnstone Engine Driver			
for Burning Kilburnies Fire Box		10	
" Hugh Smiley Engine Driver for			
disobeying Alex Mair Superintendant			
at Ayr and threatening to fight			
with the Servants at that Station		10	
. David Smiley for Same offence		10	
James Howie Engine Driver for			
Coming too quick into the Glasgow			
Station running into Marmion Engine	1		
16 James McDonald Engine Driver	1		
	11	18	4

PART 3

The Travellers

h owever important to the railway companies were industrial and commercial users, much of their planning, improvement and publicity went into passenger services, creating a whole new travelling public; going to work, on holiday, on outings and specially advertised excursions for shopping, entertainment and sightseeing. Connecting forms of transport, such as the omnibus, put the passenger's entire journey in the railway company's hands. Cheap tickets helped to widen the range of potential customers to include many who had scarcely travelled at all beyond their home neighbourhood.

Reflecting contemporary divisions, the companies provided many comforts for 1st Class passengers but for a long time the facilities offered to poorer travellers (paying less) matched the spartan character of their other daily circumstances. Rich travellers took their horsedrawn carriages on the early trains (like modern motorail) and might enjoy the privacy of a family saloon. The earliest appearance of the WC on the trains was in these private carriages. The poorer service for 3rd Class passengers prompted the introduction of a parliamentary bill in 1844 which called for all companies to run at least one train per day for 3rd Class travellers.

Early trains had no heating but footwarmers were introduced in the 1850s. Pullman coaches were introduced to Britain from America by the Midland Railway in 1874. About the same time that company abolished 2nd Class carriages and upgraded the 3rd Class. Towards the end of the century coaches were larger, better sprung and well-heated. Many a chilly wait for the train was made bearable by the waiting-room coal fire. Thousands of surviving timetables and other publicity material give some idea of the volume of traffic in the world of inter-company rivalry for customers.

41
Timetable of the Garnkirk and Glasgow Railway, 1842; for many years horsedrawn coaches, omnibuses and charabancs made connecting links for railway passengers. (BR/TT(S)/3/1/33)

The Garnkirk and Glasgow Railway was incorporated in 1826 and opened in 1831. On its extension eastwards it was renamed the Glasgow, Garnkirk and Coatbridge Railway in 1844. It was purchased by the Caledonian Railway Company, in 1846, who changed the original terminus from Glebe Street, St Rollox, to Buchanan Street Station which opened on 1 November 1849.

GARNKIRK & GLASGOW RAILWAY.

SUMMER HOURS,

From 4th APRIL to 3d OCTOBER.

THE PASSENGER TRAINS leave the DEPOT, TOWNHEAD, GLASGOW, and LEAEND DEPOT, AIRDRIE, as follows:—

FROM GLASGOW:	FROM AIRDRIE:
Quarter-past Seven, morn.	Half-past Eight, morning,
Quarter-past Ten, do.	Half-past Eleven, do.
Quarter-past One, aftern.	Half-past Two, afternoon,
Five o'clock, do.	Half-past Six, do.

INTERMEDIATE STATIONS.

COATBRIDGE to GLASGOW,	about 20 Minutes to	9, 12, 3, and 7 o'clock.
GARTSHERRIE to GLASGOW,	do. 5 Minutes to	9, 12, 3, and 7 o'clock.
GARTCOSH to GLASGOW,	do.	9, 12, 3, and 7 o'clock.
GARNKIRK WORKS to GLASGOW,	do. 5 Minutes past	9, 12, 3, and 7 o'clock.
STEPPS to GLASGOW,	do. 10 Minutes past	9, 12, 3, and 7 o'clock.

The WISHAW and COLTNESS RAILWAY COACH, from HOLYTOWN and NEWARTHILL, joins the morning Train from Gartsherrie to Glasgow, and returns with the last afternoon Train.

AN OMNIBUS FROM BRUNSWICK PLACE, TRONGATE.

☞ Passengers, whether by Omnibus or not, are requested to be at the Depôt in time to purchase Tickets and be seated in the Carriages, as the Trains will not wait beyond the specified hours of starting.

March, 1842.

Notice of the opening of the Forth Railway Bridge for passenger traffic, 5 March 1890, following its official opening by the Prince of Wales the previous day. (BR/FOR/4/3)

NORTH BRITISH RAILWAY COMPANY.

OPENING OF THE FORTH BRIDGE
FOR
PASSENGER TRAFFIC
BETWEEN
EDINBURGH & DUNFERMLINE
ON
WEDNESDAY, 5th MARCH 1890.

The Public is respectfully informed that the Forth Bridge will be opened for Passenger Traffic between Edinburgh and Dunfermline on **Wednesday, 5th March 1890**, on and after which date the present Passenger Service *via* Ratho, Port Edgar, and North Queensferry will be discontinued, and a new Service of Trains will be given *via* Ratho and the Forth Bridge at the following hours, until further notice :—

From EDINBURGH. Week Days.

Classes.	I 3 A.M	I 3 A.M.	I 3 A.M.	I 3 P.M.	I 3 P.M.	I 3 P.M.	Sat. only. I 3 P.M.
EDINBURGH (Wav. Station) dep.	6 40	9 30	11 40	2 5	4 48	7 50	10 30
Haymarket - - ,,	6 44	9 34	11 44	2 9	4 52	7 54	10 34
Corstorphine - - ,,	...	9 40	...	2 15	4 58	8 0	10 40
Gogar - - - ,,	...	9 45	...	2 20	5 3	8 6	10 46
Ratho - - - ,,	6 58	9 52	11 58	2 27	5 11	8 13	10 53
Kirkliston - - ,,	7 4	9 58	12 4	2 33	5 17	8 19	10 59
Forth Bridge Station - ,,	7 13	10 7	12 13	2 42	5 26	8 28	11 8
Inverkeithing - - ,,	7 22	10 16	12 22	2 51	5 35	8 37	11 17
DUNFERMLINE (Low. St.) arr.	7 30	10 25	12 30	3 0	5 43	8 45	11 25

To EDINBURGH. Week-Days.

Classes.	I 3 A.M.	I 3 A.M.	I 3 A.M.	I 3 P.M.	I 3 P.M.	I 3 P.M.	Sat. only. I 3 P.M.
DUNFERMLINE (Low. St.) dep.	7 45	8 30	10 45	1 45	4 25	6 35	9 10
Inverkeithing - - ,,	7 54	8 39	10 54	1 54	4 34	6 44	9 19
Forth Bridge Station - ,,	8 3	8 48	11 3	2 3	4 43	6 53	9 28
Kirkliston - - ,,	8 12	8 57	11 12	2 12	4 52	7 2	9 37
Ratho - - - ,,	8 19	9 4	11 19	2 19	4 59	7 9	9 44
Gogar - - - ,,	8 26	...	11 26	2 26	5 6	...	9 51
Corstorphine - - ,,	8 31	......	11 31	2 31	5 11	......	9 56
Haymarket - - ,,	8 37	9 17	11 37	2 37	5 17	7 22	10 2
EDINBURGH (Waverley Stn.) arr.	8 45	9 25	11 45	2 45	5 25	7 30	10 10

IMPORTANT NOTICE.
Simultaneously with the commencement of the above service, Port-Edgar Station will be entirely closed for Traffic, while North and South Queensferry and Dalmeny Stations will be used only for Goods Traffic.

QUEENSFERRY PASSAGE.

On 5th March 1890, the Sailings on the Queensferry Passage will be altered to the following, which will remain in force until further notice, viz. :—

		Week-Days.						Sundays.		
		A.M.	A.M.	A.M.	P.M.	P.M.	P.M.	P.M.	A.M.	P.M.	P.M.
New Halls - - - depart	8 0	9 0	11 0	1 0	3 30	5 0	6 0	8 30	1 15	5 0
North Queensferry (Old Pier) arrive	8 12	9 12	11 12	1 12	3 42	5 12	6 12	8 42	1 27	5 12
		A.M.	A.M.	A.M.	P.M.	P.M.	P.M.	P.M.	A.M.	P.M.	P.M.
North Queensferry (Old Pier) depart	7 30	8 25	10 0	12 30	2 30	4 30	5 30	8 0	12 30	3 30
New Halls - - - arrive	7 42	8 37	10 12	12 42	2 42	4 42	5 42	8 12	12 42	3 42

6-30 a.m. Train from GLASGOW (Queen Street High Level) to EDINBURGH.

The 6-30 a.m. Train from Glasgow (Queen Street High Level) to Edinburgh will cease calling at Gogar and Corstorphine, and will be accelerated so as to arrive at Haymarket at 8-27 and Edinburgh (Waverley Station) at 8-35 a.m.

EDINBURGH, *March* 1890.   (2-M)   **J. WALKER, General Manager.**

BY N. B. R. TRAIN.

CIRCULAR TOUR No. 16.

21   FIRST CLASS and CABIN.—Fare_____   **21**

FOR 45 DAME STREET, DUBLIN OFFICE, C. & S. 12.

Agents will please date with ink, or stamp, each Coupon before issuing, and take great care to sell from the top, IN CONSECUTIVE ORDER.

In selling one of these Tickets to a Child, the Agent may cut it right down the centre of all the Coupons from top to bottom, keeping the other half, and non-issuing or selling it afterwards, as case may be.

Issued for *North British Railway* subject to conditions in Time Tables and Tourist Programmes. Through Tickets, in cases where Journey is not continuous, do not include cost of transfer between Railway Termini in Towns, or between Railway Stations and Steamboats.

(C. & S. 12.)   **21**   AVAILABLE BETWEEN   **21**   (C. & S. 12.)

N. B. R. P. T.   **GLASGOW**   N. B. R. P. T.

CIRCULAR TOUR, No. 16.   (Queen St., Bellgrove or College Stns.) AND (Queen St., Bellgrove or College Stns.)   CIRCULAR TOUR, No. 16.

EDINBURGH (*North*) to Granton, Broughty, Montrose, Aberdeen, Keith, Fochabers, Elgin, Inverness, Caledonian Canal, Fort-William, Ballachulish (for Glencoe), Oban, Firth of Clyde, Glasgow, and Back, *or vice versa.*

EDINBURGH, (Waverley Station)   (Waverley Station)

Single Journey either way.

1st. FIRST CLASS. 1st.
Holder can break Journey at any stopping station.

EDINBURGH (*North*) to Granton, Broughty, Montrose, Aberdeen, Keith, Fochabers, Elgin, Inverness, Caledonian Canal, Fort-William, Ballachulish (for Glencoe), Oban, Firth of Clyde, Glasgow, and Back, *or vice versa.*

Issued for *North British Railway* subject to conditions in Time Tables and Tourist Programmes. Through Tickets, in cases where Journey is not continuous, do not include cost of Transfer between Railway Termini in Towns, or between Railway Stations and Steamboats.

(C. & S. 12.)   **21**   AVAILABLE BETWEEN   **21**   (C. & S. 12.)

N. B. R. P. T.   **OBAN**   N. B. R. P. T.

CIRCULAR TOUR, No. 16.   (Argyleshire)   AND   (Argyleshire)   CIRCULAR TOUR, No. 16.

EDINBURGH (*North*) to Granton, Broughty, Montrose, Aberdeen, Keith, Fochabers, Elgin, Inverness, Caledonian Canal, Fort-William, Ballachulish (for Glencoe), Oban, Firth of Clyde, Glasgow, and Back, *or vice versa.*

GLASGOW, (Broomielaw)   (Broomielaw)

Via Crinan Canal or Mull of Kintyre,
Cabin of Mr. D. MacBrayne's Steamers. Cabin.
Single Journey either way.

Holder can break Journey at any stopping place, and, if preferred, can travel between Dunoon, Cowlairs and Glasgow (Queen St. Station), via Craigendoran Pier, Helensburgh, joining or leaving Royal Mail Steamer at Dunoon.

EDINBURGH (*North*) to Granton, Broughty, Montrose, Aberdeen, Keith, Fochabers, Elgin, Inverness, Caledonian Canal, Fort-William, Ballachulish (for Glencoe), Oban, Firth of Clyde, Glasgow, and Back, *or vice versa.*

Issued for *North British Railway* subject to conditions in Time Tables and Tourist Programmes. Through Tickets, in cases where Journey is not continuous, do not include cost of Transfer between Railway Termini in Towns, or between Railway Stations and Steamboats.

(C. & S. 12.)   **21**   AVAILABLE BETWEEN   **21**   (C. & S. 12.)

N. B. R. P. T.   **FORT-WILLIAM,**   N. B. R. P. T.

CIRCULAR TOUR, No. 16.   **BALLACHULISH (for Glencoe)**   CIRCULAR TOUR, No. 16.

EDINBURGH (*North*) to Granton, Broughty, Montrose, Aberdeen, Keith, Fochabers, Elgin, Inverness, Caledonian Canal, Fort-William, Ballachulish (for Glencoe), Oban, Firth of Clyde, Glasgow, and Back, *or vice versa.*

AND
OBAN, (Oban)   (Oban)

Cabin of Mr. D. MacBrayne's Steamer. Cabin.
Single Journey either way.
Holder can break Journey at any stopping pier.

EDINBURGH (*North*) to Granton, Broughty, Montrose, Aberdeen, Keith, Fochabers, Elgin, Inverness, Caledonian Canal, Fort-William, Ballachulish (for Glencoe), Oban, Firth of Clyde, Glasgow, and Back, *or vice versa.*

Issued for *North British Railway* subject to conditions in Time Tables and Tourist Programmes. Through Tickets, in cases where Journey is not continuous, do not include cost of Transfer between Railway Termini in Towns, or between Railway Stations and Steamboats.

(C. & S. 12.)   **21**   AVAILABLE BETWEEN   **21**   (C. & S. 12.)

N. B. R. P. T.   **INVERNESS,**   N. B. R. P. T.

CIRCULAR TOUR, No. 16.   **FOYERS and**   CIRCULAR TOUR, No. 16.

EDINBURGH (*North*) to Granton, Broughty, Montrose, Aberdeen, Keith, Fochabers, Elgin, Inverness, Caledonian Canal, Fort-William, Ballachulish (for Glencoe), Oban, Firth of Clyde, Glasgow, and Back, *or vice versa.*

FORT-WILLIAM,
Via CALEDONIAN CANAL.
Cabin of Mr. D. MacBrayne's Steamer. Cabin.
Single Journey either way.
Holder can break Journey at any stopping pier.

EDINBURGH (*North*) to Granton, Broughty, Montrose, Aberdeen, Keith, Fochabers, Elgin, Inverness, Caledonian Canal, Fort-William, Ballachulish (for Glencoe), Oban, Firth of Clyde, Glasgow, and Back, *or vice versa.*

Issued for *North British Railway* subject to conditions in Time Tables and Tourist Programmes. Through Tickets, in cases where Journey is not continuous, do not include cost of Transfer between Railway Termini in Towns, or between Railway Stations and Steamboats.

(C. & S. 12.)   **21**   AVAILABLE BETWEEN   **21**   (C. & S. 12.)

N. B. R. P. Train.   **EDINBURGH**   N. B. R. P. Train.

CIRCULAR TOUR, No. 16.   (Waverley Station)   AND   (Waverley Station)   CIRCULAR TOUR, No. 16.

EDINBURGH (*North*) to Granton, Broughty, Montrose, Aberdeen, Keith, Fochabers, Elgin, Inverness, Caledonian Canal, Fort-William, Ballachulish (for Glencoe), Oban, Firth of Clyde, Glasgow, and Back, *or vice versa.*

INVERNESS (Highland Railway)   (Highland Railway)

Via Granton, Broughty, Montrose, Aberdeen, Keith, Fochabers & Elgin.

Single Journey either way.

1st. FIRST CLASS. 1st.
Holder can break Journey at any stopping station and travel from Ladybank to Perth and Back free.

EDINBURGH (*North*) to Granton, Broughty, Montrose, Aberdeen, Keith, Fochabers, Elgin, Inverness, Caledonian Canal, Fort-William, Ballachulish (for Glencoe), Oban, Firth of Clyde, Glasgow, and Back, *or vice versa.*

43
Specimen tickets for associated train and steamer services.
(BR/GEN(S)/3/1)

Timetables and other publicity issued by
various railway companies offering
holiday services to Scotland, particularly
to the Highlands, 1898-1907.
(BR/LIB(S)/18/22; BR/TT(S)/3/2/13;
BR/LIB(S)/19/36; BR/TT(S)/3/2/6;
BR/LIB(S)/18/34)

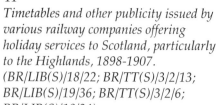

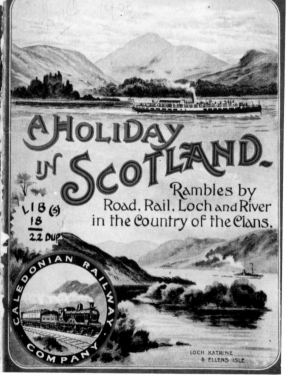

KAL GUIDE TO·

IGHLANDS
LAND

OUTE·

LOCH LOMOND
LOCH AWE
& OBAN

ARK·

STREET
GOW·

AGENTS·

LIST OF FURNISHED
Lodgings

IN FARM HOUSES, COUNTRY VILLAGES
& OTHER PLACES IN THE DISTRICT
SERVED BY THE
HIGHLAND RAILWAY

THE
HIGHLAND
RAILWAY
COMPANY

SEASON 1902

The to Scotland's Beauties.

NORTH BRITISH RAILWAY

45
Highland Railway: holidaymakers arriving at Inverness Station off the London train, undated [early 20th century]. (BR/HR/4/27)

Travellers' tales from the 19th century remind us that people might experience discomfort and frustration as well as pleasure and excitement on the Victorian railways.

46

A letter of March 1886 describes the plight of snowbound passengers:
  '*The snowed up passengers in trains suffered dreadfully and had to drink the water out of the foot-warmers!! They had found some herring in the van and cooked them at the engine fire on the stoker's shovel, perhaps this caused the thirst'. (Collection of Murray, Beith and Murray, WS: GD.374/14/15)*

47

From a pamphlet entitled 'Citizens Save the Gardens', about what the North British and Caledonian Railway Companies were doing in their rival attempts to utilise the Waverley Market site in central Edinburgh. It quoted an irate writer who described the rush-hour at Waverley Station about 1890:
  '*On the platforms of Waverley Station at Edinburgh may be witnessed every evening in summer a scene of confusion so chaotic that a sober description of it is incredible to those who have not themselves survived it …'.*
(Collection of Dundas and Wilson, CS: GD.282/13/259)

These sentiments were echoed in E. Foxwell and T. C. Farrer Express Trains English and Foreign *(London, 1889), before the opening of the Forth Bridge and the subsequent alterations at Waverley Station:*
  '*Trains of caravan length come in portentously late from Perth, so that each is mistaken for its successor; these have to be broken up and re-made on insufficient sidings, while bewildered crowds of tourists sway up and down amongst equally bewildered porters on the narrow village platform reserved for these most important expresses; the higher officials stand lost in subtle thought, returning now and then to repeated inquiries some masterpiece of reply couched in the cautious conditional, while the hands of the clock with a humorous air survey the abandoned sight, till at length, without any obvious reason and with sudden stealth, the shame-stricken driver hurries his packed passengers off into the dark. Once off, the driver and the engine do much to make us forget the disgraceful rout from which we have just emerged'.*

THROUGH FARES TO EDINBURGH
1st Class Rail 10d 2nd Class Rail 8d
and InsideCoach. and InsideCoach.

NORTH BRITISH RAILWAY COMPANY.

48
*Eager travellers aboard a North British
Railway Company horse-bus at Edenhall
near Musselburgh, undated.
(BR/LIB(S)/6/224)*

Notice of the Caledonian Railway Company advertising an excursion from Edinburgh to the Banks of Clyde – leaving at 6 am, 1848. Excursions, at cheap rates, encouraged the less well-to-do to use the railways. (BR/CAL/4/7)

PLEASURE EXCURSION
TO THE
BANKS OF CLYDE.

THE EDINBURGH LANARK AND BIGGAR CLUBS
Respectfully announce to their friends th   they hav made arrangements for a

PLEASURE EXCURSION TO LANARK AND BIGGAR,
BY THE CALEDONIAN RAILWAY,
On THURSDAY, the 8th of JUNE, 1848,
The day on which the Yearly Ceremony of Riding the Land Marches, called the "Lan'imers," is observed at Lanark.

The Train will leave the Edinburgh Terminus, Lothian Road, at Six o'clock A.M.   At Carstairs Junction, one Division of it will proceed to the Lanark Station, and another at the same time to Symington for Biggar, each arriving at its respective Station about Half-past Seven o'clock.   The Trains will start on their return from Lanark and Symington Stations at Nine P.M.—thus allowing *Thirteen* Hours for rural recreation, angling in the Clyde, or surveying the remarkable objects and splendid scenery in the different localities.

Visitors to LANARK, after inspecting that Royal Burgh—remarkable for its antiquity, and its connection with some very interesting passages in the life of Wallace, and the proceedings of the Covenanters—are recommended to proceed to the finely ornamented and romantic Grounds of BONNITON, to which free access has been readily and kindly granted on this occasion.   After passing the gates they should repair to the Pavilion, situated on a lofty sloping bank opposite

THE FALL AND THE ANCIENT CASTLE OF COREHOUSE,
where, in mirrors suspended around the walls, are presented some very singular and almost terrific views of the foaming Cataract below.

BONNITON FALL
should next be visited, where the River above is seen flowing along with its usual placidity, and then almost at once bursting over a precipice thirty-two feet high, and at the same time forming an island, to which access can be got by an elegant iron bridge.   Returning by the lower walks, the River is seen at one time rolling its waters along a spacious channel o'erhung by lofty woods and perpendicular cliffs a hundred feet in height, and at another pent up amid rugged precipices, till it is contracted to a breadth not exceeding eight feet.   A little below, every advantageous view is obtained of one of the most sublime scenes in Europe—

"Where ancient Corehouse hangs above the str | With giddy heads we view the dreadful deep,
And far beneath the trembling surges gleam ; | And cattle snort and tremble at the steep,
Engulph'd in crags the fretting river raves, | Where down at once the foaming waters pour,
Chafed into foam, resound his tortured waves. | And tott'ring rocks repel the deafening roar."—*Wilson.*

CORRA LINN consists of three different Falls, and is altogether eighty-four feet high.   Leaving the Woods of Bonniton,

THE COTTON MILLS OF NE   LANARK,
built in 1785 by David Dale, should next receive a visit.   Their lebrity has extended over the world, not les from their connection with the famous Mr Robert Owen, than from their romantic situation and the excellence of their manufactures and internal arrangements.—Returning to Lanark, parties may next visit the

FALL OF STONEBYRES, and the CHASM OF CARTLANE CRAGS.
Stonebyres Fall, two miles below Lanark, though destitute of some of the artificial accessories of the Fall of Corehouse, is allowed rather to exceed it in some points of savage sublimity.   It also consists of three distinct leaps, and is altogether eighty-two feet in height.   A short distance above it, the channel of the River is contracted to a few feet, while immediately below is the celebrated "SALMON POOL," from which salmon are frequently seen to make desperate but unavailing efforts to spring up the raging cataract.   By the kind permission of the proprietor, Sir N man Macdonald Lockhart, Bart., the whole of the splendid and romantic grounds of Lee will be thrown open, and everything done to promote the gratification   They will thus have ample liberty to inspect the celebrated "PEAS TREE," measuring forty-seven feet in circumference and sixty feet in height, and containing a cavity that can admit ten grown persons, and in which Oliver Cromwell and a party of his friends once dined ; and also to explore the wonders of CARTLANE CRAGS—a precipitous chasm four hundred feet deep, traversed by the River Mouss, and evidently formed by some convulsion of nature, as every recess on the one side has a corresponding projection on the other—the whole presenting a frightful aspect of wood, crag, and precipice, and fully realising the description of it by Joanna Baillie, when she says that it presents

"Wall above wall, half-veil'd, half-seen, | With jagged breach, and rift, and scaur,
The pendent folds of wood between, | Like the scorch'd wreck of ancient war."

The lower extremity of this Ravine is spanned by an elegant bridge, built in 1822, consisting of three arches of the stupendous height of 136 feet.   Above the Bridge is WALLACE'S CAVE and the remains of an ancient Castle called "QUA," and below is the OLD BRIDGE, which is supposed to have stood from the time of the Picts or the Romans.   Among the many Gentlemen's Seats in this neighbourhood, none will be viewed with greater interest than the old castellated MANSION OF JERVISWOOD, the residence of Robert Baillie, who suffered martyrdom during the bloody and tyrannical reign of Charles II.

Those who prefer going to SYMINGTON, may agreeably employ their time either in ascending

TINTO HILL
in the immediate neighbourhood, which rises to the height of 2336 feet, and commands a prospect that embraces a portion of SIXTEEN DIFFERENT COUNTIES, and extends from the Cheviot Mountains to the Grampians, and from the Bass Rock to the rugged and towering peaks of Arran, while the whole of the fertile and populous district of Clydesdale is spread out below like a map ; or in visiting the Town of BIGGAR, where the PARISH CHURCH, built in 1545 by Malcolm Lord Fleming,—the MOAT KNOWE, a Station of the Romans,—the site and some remaining fragments of BOGHALL CASTLE, the ancient seat of the distinguished family of Fleming,—and the Plains on which Wallace gained a decisive victory over the English in 1297, will be found not unworthy of attention.

The party to Biggar will be met at some distance from the town by a Procession of the Inhabitants, accompanied by a Band of Music, and a Presentation of Prizes to the Schools of Biggar, by the Edinburgh Biggar Club, will take place in the North United Presbyterian Church, at Half-past 11 o'clock—Mr James Tweedie, President, in the Chair.

A PUBLIC BREAKFAST will take place at LANARK, in the CLYDESDALE INN, at 9 A.M., Tickets 1s. 6d. each; and at BIGGAR, in the CROWN INN, at 9 A.M., Tickets, 1s. 3d. each.

FARES, GOING AND RETURNING :
To LANARK, Second Class, 5s. ; Third Class, 2s. 8d.—To SYMINGTON, Second Class, 6s. ; Third Class, 3s.
CHILDREN UNDER TWELVE YEARS OF AGE, HALF FARE.

Tickets may be had from Mr Thomas Lawrie, 136 Nicolson Street ; Mr William Gibson, 1 Lothian Street ; Mr A. D. Campbell, 58 South Bridge ; Mr William Anderson, at Mr Bell's, 86 South Bridge ; Mr James Marr, 11 East Register Street ; Mr R. S. Hamilton, 13 Rose Street ; Mr James Tweedie, 21 George Street ; Mr Thomas Breckenridge, Customhouse, Shrub Place, Leith Walk ; Reid & Son, 36 Shore, Leith ; or from any Member of the Committees of the Edinburgh Lanark and Biggar Clubs.

J. HOGG, Printer, 56 & 122 Nicolson Street.

B.T.C. ARCHIVES

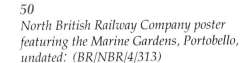

50
North British Railway Company poster featuring the Marine Gardens, Portobello, undated: (BR/NBR/4/313)

NORTH BRITISH RAILWAY

COME WHEN YOU LIKE, GO WHEN YOU LIKE

ASK FOR OUR Special Book Coupons ADMIT YOU **6 SHOWS 1/**

Gardens Open FROM **10.30 a.m.** TO **10.30 p.m**

Scotland's Pleasure City by the Silvery Sea

THEATRE—ADMISSION FREE

6D.
BY TRAIN
INCLUDES FARE AND ADMISSION

GRAND EXHIBITION & CARNIVAL HALLS—ADMISSION FREE

Special Performances Twice Daily

ALL THE LEADING

LOND and PROVINCIAL ARTISTES

In Ever Changing Program

THE EMPRESS BALLROOM—ADMISSION FREE

Musical Promenade Concerts
Ye Ancient Scottish Fair
Working Exhibits
Fanning's Marionettes
The Merrymakers
High-Class Restaurants

SPORTS GROUND—ADMISSION FREE

12 HOURS 12 FUN AND FROLIC

MOUNTAIN SLIDE AND FUN CITY

Band Contests
Military Displays
Football Matches and Sports

WEDNESDAY and SATURDAY—
GRAND
FIREWORK PRODUCTIONS
ADMISSION - FREE

BAND STAND AND PROMENADE

All the LEADING MILITARY BANDS, Afternoon & Evening

The Great Joy Wheel
The Foolish House
Figure 8   River Caves
Hibbert's Electric Theatre
Enchanted Castle
Flying Machine

And 100 AMUSEMENT DEVICES

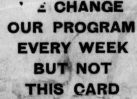

SCENIC RAILWAY

CHANGE OUR PROGRAM EVERY WEEK BUT NOT THIS CARD

SCOTLAND'S GREAT ZOO—ADMISSION

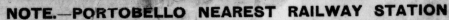

NOTE.—PORTOBELLO NEAREST RAILWAY STATION

Special Railway Return Tickets, including Admission, from Edinburgh (Waverley) and any Suburban S.

SERVICE SEE N.B. RAILWAY TIME TABLES

7

51

London and North Eastern Railway staff notice about the maintenance of fires in the waiting rooms of stations, undated. (BR/LNE/4/454)

52

Plan of offices for Killiecrankie Station, Perthshire, 1896. Drawings of railway buildings for the use of passengers, staff, or the housing and maintenance of locomotives and rolling stock and the storage of goods are fine examples of the draughtsman's art. (Register House Plans: 15166)

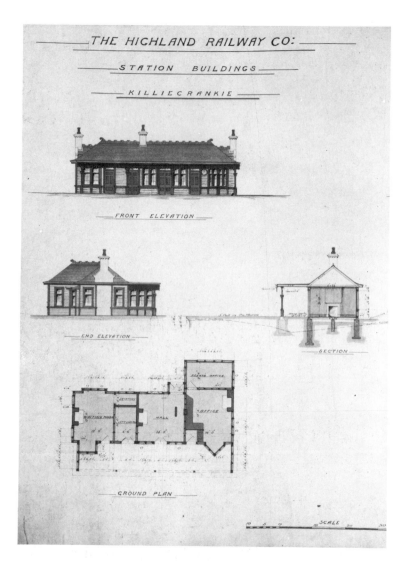

THE LONDON & NORTH EASTERN RAILWAY

Preparation and Maintenance of Fires in Railway Waiting Rooms

For the better service and greater comfort of the travelling public members of the staff charged with the duty of attending to waiting-room fires should observe the following simple directions for lighting and replenishing them. With a little care waiting-room fires can be kept bright and cheerful without excessive consumption of coal, and so contribute to the health and pleasure of passengers and to the good appearance of the stations.

To ensure a cheerful and yet economical fire :—

(1) The ashes should be raked out and removed from the grate before preparing the new fire.

(2) A small quantity of paper should be placed in the *centre* of the grate and covered with small pieces of wood, so arranged that a free circulation of air can take place.

(3) Upon the wood place first the unconsumed coal from the old fire and upon this small pieces of new coal.

(4) Light the paper and when the coal has become well alight the fire should be built up to the requisite size with lumps placed so that a free circulation of air can take place. The best size of coal is about 4 inches cube.

(5) Replenishing the fire should be done before the fire gets too low. The reason for this is that sufficient heat must remain in the fire in order to ensure that the tarry matter in the new coal shall be heated as quickly as possible so that it may give flame. It is important to use up all small coal and slack that has been formed in the stove. This should be placed at the back of the fire in small quantities at a time. When replenishing the fire the ashes which have accumulated should be raked out to enable a free circulation of air to pass through the grate.

(6) A fire covered with raw black coal gives no heat, and this can only be avoided by replenishing the fire regularly, and in the end fuel economy is best effected by stoking little and often and keeping the fire free of ashes.

(7) See that the doors of the waiting room are kept closed as far as possible.

G. MILLS,
Divisional General Manager,
Scottish Area.

Early attempts by the railway companies to run steamboats were failures partly due to the opposition of private steamship companies. In the later 19th century in the north-west competition came mainly from the firm of David MacBrayne whose fleet of vessels reached its maximum of 36 in 1912.

The most successful railway fleets were those run by the various Steam Packet Companies, notably, those of the North British, with its headquarters at Craigendoran from 1882, and the Caledonian, operating out of Gourock from 1889.

Railway steamers also operated on east coast routes, carrying revenue-earning freight as well as passengers. Rail and steamer linked tours were a popular type of holiday and also a means of enjoying a one-day local fair holiday. The names of well-known paddle-steamers - Glen Sannox, Talisman, Waverley and Jeanie Deans - have passed into the legends of travel.

53
The PS 'William Muir' disembarking passengers at Burntisland pier, undated. (BR/GEN(S)/3/6)

54
The Glasgow and South Western Railway Company PS 'Glen Sannox'; the first paddle-steamer of this name built in 1892, undated. (BR/GEN(S)/3/75)

The first royal train journey in Scotland took place unscheduled when on 29 September 1848, Aberdeen harbour being fogbound, the proposed cruise south in the royal yacht by Queen Victoria and Prince Albert had to be abandoned. At 30 minutes' notice the Aberdeen Railway provided a 1st Class carriage for the Queen and the Prince Consort who then accomplished the longest royal train journey to date: 500 miles from Aberdeen to Euston. The Queen's very first train journey had taken place in 1842 from Slough (for Windsor) to Paddington Station.

Later in her long reign Queen Victoria made regular journeys from London or Windsor to Ballater (for Balmoral), sometimes accompanied by guests as well as members of her family and household.

55
Arrangements of carriages by the London and North Western Railway for Queen Victoria, her family and household on their journey from Gosport to Ballater in the autumn of 1899. (BR/HRP(S)/3/14)

56
Queen Victoria and Prince Albert about to leave Cambridge for London by train in 1847. (Illustrated London News)

LONDON AND NORTH WESTERN RAILWAY.

ARRANGEMENT OF CARRIAGES

COMPOSING

HER MAJESTY'S TRAIN

FROM GOSPORT TO BALLATER,

ON THURSDAY, THE 31ST AUGUST, AND FRIDAY, THE 1ST SEPTEMBER, 1899.

ENGINE.	GUARD.	FOR MEN SERVANTS.	FOR PAGES AND UPPER SERVANTS.	DRESSERS AND LADIES' MAIDS.	PRINCE MAURICE OF BATTENBERG AND ATTENDANTS. — MISS BOWER.	DOWAGER LADY CHURCHILL. HON. HARRIET PHIPPS. MISS HUGHES.	PRINCESS VICTORIA EUGENIE OF BATTENBERG. MDLLE. DU PERRUT. PRINCES ALEXANDER AND LEOPOLD OF BATTENBERG. MR. THEOBALD.	PRINCES EDWARD, ALBERT, AND PRINCESS VICTORIA OF YORK AND ATTENDANTS.	QUEEN'S DRESSERS.	Her Majesty AND PRINCESS HENRY OF BATTENBERG.	PERSONAL SERVANTS.	LIEUT.-COL. DAVIDSON. COL. D. BROWNE. SIR JAMES REID. *SIR J. MCNEILL.	INDIAN ATTENDANTS.	DIRECTORS.	DIRECTORS.	FOURGON. (To be attached at Basingstoke.)	GUARD.
ENGINE.	VAN. No. 210.	CARRIAGE No. 870.	SALOON. No. 72.	SALOON. No. 73.	SALOON. No. 1.	SALOON. No. 153.	SALOON. No. 56.	SALOON. No. 50.		Royal Saloon.		SALOON. No. 131.	SALOON. No. 71.	SALOON. No. 180.	CARRIAGE No. 306.	TRUCK. No. 100.	VAN. No. 272.

< ———————— 362 feet 8 inches ———————— > < ———————— 269 feet 5 inches ———————— >

* Leaves Train at Basingstoke.

57
Car used by the Highland Railway Company to advertise fishing holidays by rail. The railway companies were very publicity conscious and had a flair for effective advertising. 1908 or after. (BR/HR/4/30/2)

*The North British Station Hotel,
Edinburgh, photographed shortly after its
opening in 1902. The railway hotels,
particularly those sited in major British
cities, were veritable palaces, advertising
the scale of the companies' operations and
the standard of service to prosperous
railway travellers. (BR/LIB(S)/6/224)*

PART 4

The trains

Central to the whole operation were the engines, rudimentary in construction to start with but increasingly powerful, efficient and safe. Changes in design were largely dictated by considerations of cost and efficiency and the competitive atmosphere in which the companies operated. Companies were anxious that their trains should look well in addition to performing efficiently. Thousands of diagrams and drawings bear testimony to the skills of the railway designers and draughtsmen and the many photographs and surviving steam engines demonstrate those of the builders. Countless railwaymen over the generations have been photographed with the engines of which they and their companies were so proud and which have remained at the heart of enthusiasm for railway history.

As locomotives developed in power the designers had to think hard about safety. Increasing numbers of trains serving industry as well as the public meant the need for more reliable methods of braking, signalling and traffic control. Although there were countless small mishaps to the travelling public, and to staff who sometimes ignored the advice of the companies' rule books, the number of serious accidents has to be set alongside the thousands of train journeys that took place; the result is a fairly good record of safe travel. However, two of the worst accidents in British railway history, that on the Tay Bridge (1879) and that at Quintinshill, Gretna (1915) took place in Scotland.

59
North British Railway employees and 0-6-0 locomotive No 155 at Anstruther, Fife, 1887. (BR/NBR/5/77)

60
Wigtownshire Railway locomotive No 5, rebuilt as 0-6-0 tank engine, 1885, photographed with staff at Garlieston Station, c.1890. (D L Smith Collection: GD.422/8/74)

61

Highland Railway: diagram of 4-6-0 goods engine. Designed by David Jones and built in 1894 by Sharp, Stewart and Co Ltd, Glasgow, the 'Jones Goods' was the first British 4-6-0 type to enter service. (BR/HR/5/1)

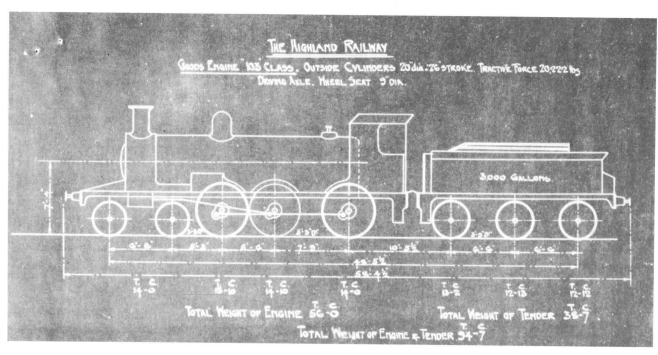

62

London and North Eastern Railway locomotive works, Inverurie: the erecting shop sometime before 1934. (BR/GNS/4/47)

63
A 2-2-2 passenger engine built about 1840 and used on the Scottish Central Railway, from an album of photographs of engines 1837-1916. Locomotive Superintendent Alexander Allan. (BR/CAL/5/22)

2-2-2 locomotive No. 57 built for the
Edinburgh and Glasgow Railway
Company by Beyer Peacock in 1856,
photographed by Thomas Annan of
Glasgow c.1862. (BR/EGR/5/1)

65
*Managers and foremen at Hyde Park
Locomotive Works, Springburn, 1863.
Photograph by George Graham.
(Courtesy of the Mitchell Library,
Glasgow.)*

W-10-8

Part of the impressive layout of the locomotive and carriage repair workshops of the London Midland and Scottish Railway, St Rollox, Glasgow, 1932. (BR/LIB(S)/15/54)

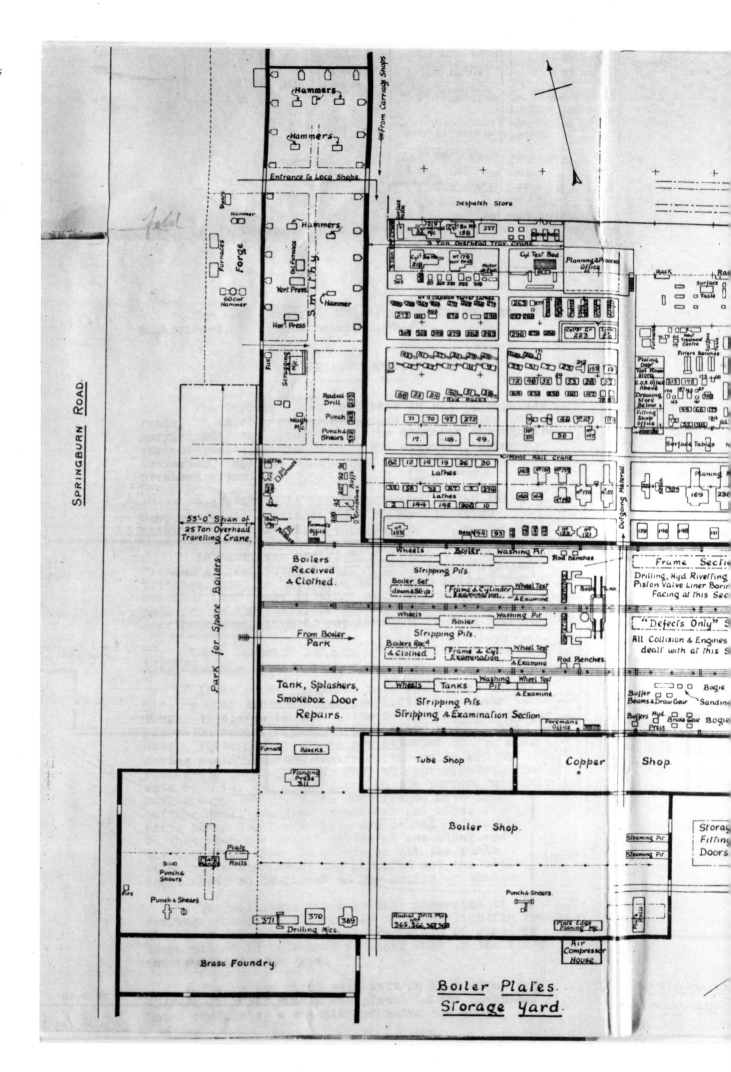

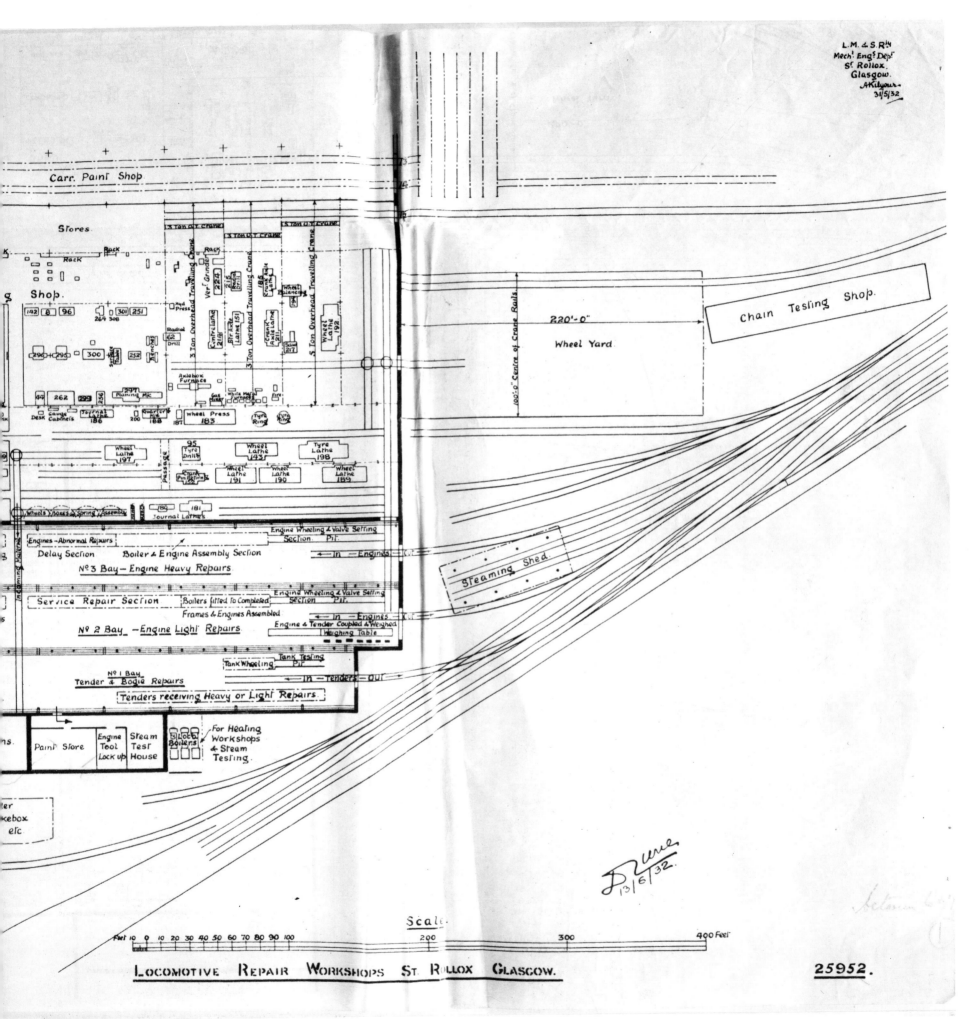

L.M. & S. R^{ly}
Mech^l Eng^s Dept
St Rollox,
Glasgow.
A.Kilgour.
31/5/32

Carr. Paint Shop

Stores

3 Ton O.T. Crane
3 Ton O.T. Crane
5 Ton O.H. Crane

Rack
Rack

Shop.

Rack

3 Ton Overhead Travelling Crane

5 Ton Overhead Travelling Crane

5 Ton Overhead Travelling Crane

142 8 96
301 251
264 308

Vert Grinder
224
216
Radial

185
Crank Axle
Lathe

Wheel
Balancing
194

Hyd
Press

Wheel Yard

220'-0"

Chain Testing Shop.

Centre Lathe
219

Str Ratio
Lathe 151

Crank
Axle Lathe
211

Wheel
Lathe
192

100'-0" Centre of Crane Rails

296 295
300
252

Surface
Plates

Radial
Drill
62

262 293 256
297 Planing M/c

Axlebox
Furnace

Gas
Furnace

White Metal
Furnace

Fire

Sam
217

Desk Gauge Cabinets

Journal
Lathe 186

200

Quarters
188

187

Wheel Press
183

Tyre
Ring

Tyre
Ring

Wheel
Lathe
197

95
Tyre
Drill

Wheel
Lathe
193

Tyre
Lathe
198

Passage

Crank
Pin Setting
186

Wheel
Lathe
191

Wheel
Lathe
190

Wheel
Lathe
189

Wheels / Axles / & Spring / Assembly.

186
181
Journal Lathes

Engine Wheeling & Valve Setting
Section. Pit.

Engines - Abnormal Repairs

Delay Section   Boiler & Engine Assembly Section

← In — Engines — Out

Nº 3 Bay — Engine Heavy Repairs

In Steaming Material

Service Repair Section   Boilers fitted to Completed

Engine Wheeling & Valve Setting
Section. Pit.

Frames & Engines Assembled

← In — Engines — Out

Nº 2 Bay — Engine Light Repairs

Engine & Tender Coupled & Weighed
Weighing Table

Steaming Shed.

Tank Testing
Pit

Tank Wheeling

Nº 1 Bay
Tender & Bogie Repairs

← In — Tenders — Out

Tenders receiving Heavy or Light Repairs

Paint Store

Engine
Tool
Lock up

Steam
Test
House

3 Loco
Boilers

For Heating
Workshops
& Steam
Testing.

Firebox
etc

13/6/32

Scale.

Feet 10 0 10 20 30 40 50 60 70 80 90 100   200   300   400 Feet

LOCOMOTIVE REPAIR WORKSHOPS ST. ROLLOX GLASGOW.

25952.

67
Trains for export: a delegation of Chinese mandarins at the North British Locomotive Company Works, Springburn, Glasgow, undated. (W E Boyd Collection: GD.257/2/47. Courtesy of the Mitchell Library, Glasgow)

68
*North British Railway 4-4-0 locomotive
No 359 'Dirk Hatteraick' on the Lothian
Coast Express, undated. (BR/NBR/5/37)*

69
*Mail and newspaper deliveries speeded up
enormously with the coming of the
railways. London and North Eastern
Railway 6-wheel van No 3251 for use on
'The Scotsman' newspaper train,
undated. (BR/LNE/5/173)*

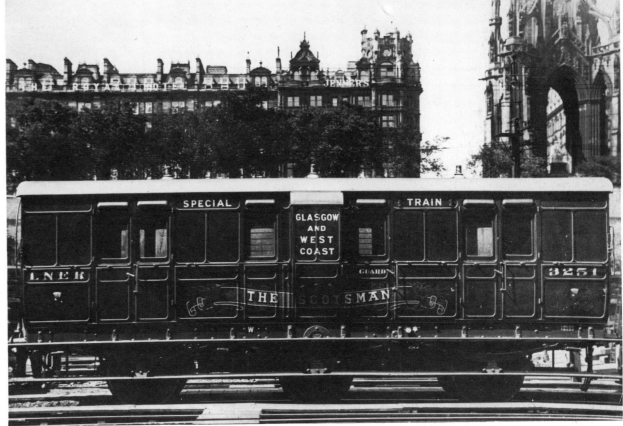

The Tay Bridge disaster, 28 December 1879; telegram sent by the Stationmaster at Dundee to the North British Railway Company's Engineer at Portobello on the night of the disaster – 'Terrible accident on Bridge ... am not quite sure as to the safety of the last train down from Edinburgh'. (Miscellaneous Collections: GD.1/556/8)

71
*Like a horseman and his 'faithful steed':
driver Anthony Ross of Ayr
photographed at Dalrymple Junction
with locomotive No 308, built by Dubs
and Company for the Glasgow and South
Western Railway in 1892. (Collection of
D L Smith: GD.422/8/68)*

72
*The end of an era: British Railways stock
book, with annotation recording the
withdrawal of the last Scottish Region
steam locomotive in 1967.
(BR/RSR/5/85)*

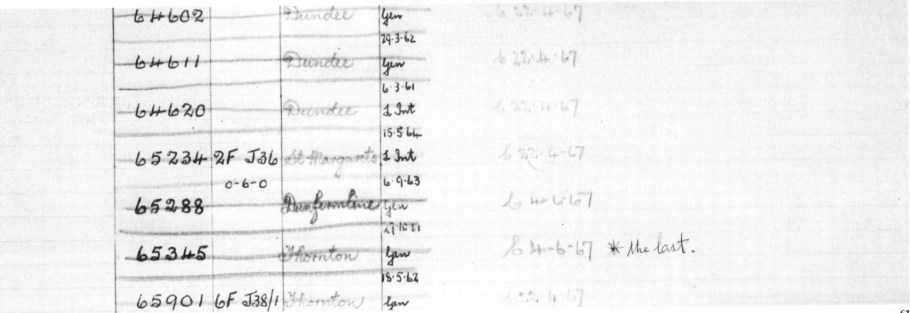

73

Personal memento of the railway: an LMS towel, removed by a Royal Marine and returned by him after the Second World War inscribed with the names of those places where he had served.
(BR/HRP(S)/77/5)

Issued for *North British Railway* subject to conditions in Time Tables and Tourist Programmes.
Through Tickets, in cases where journey is not continuous, do not include cost of transfer between
Railway Termini in Towns, or between Railway Stations and Steamboats.

(C. & S. 12.)	AVAILABLE BETWEEN	(C. & S. 12.)
N. B. R. T. 21		21 N. B. R. T.

GLASGOW

CIRCULAR TOUR, (Queen St., Bellgrove or College Stns.) AND (Queen St., Bellgrove or College Stns.) CIRCULAR TOUR,
No. 16. No. 16.

EDINBURGH,

EDINBURGH (Waverley Station) (Waverley Station) EDINBURGH
(North) to (North) to
Granton, Broughty, *Single Journey either way.* Granton, Broughty,
Montrose, Montrose,
Aberdeen, Keith, Aberdeen, Keith,
Fochabers, Elgin, **1st. FIRST CLASS. 1st.** Fochabers, Elgin,
Inverness, Caledonian Inverness, Caledonian
Canal, Fort-William, Canal, Fort-William,
Ballachulish (for Holder can break Journey at any Ballachulish (for
Glencoe), Oban, stopping station. Glencoe), Oban,
Firth of Clyde, Firth of Clyde,
Glasgow, Glasgow,
and Back *or vice versa.* and Back *or vice versa.*

**HMSO**

HMSO publications are available from:

HMSO Bookshops
71 Lothian Road, Edinburgh EH3 9AZ 031-228 4181
49 High Holborn, London WC1V 6HB 071-873 0011 (counter service only)
258 Broad Street, Birmingham B1 2HE 021-643 3740
Southey House, 33 Wine Street, Bristol BS1 2BQ 0272 264306
9-21 Princes Street, Manchester, M60 8AS 061-834 7201
80 Chichester Street, Belfast BT1 4JY 0232 238451

HMSO Publications Centre
(Mail and telephone orders only)
PO Box 276, London, SW8 5DT
Telephone orders 071-873 9090
General enquiries 071-873 0011
(queuing system in operation for both numbers)

HMSO's Accredited Agents
(see Yellow Pages)

And through good book sellers